T0079255

...roduction

VERY SHORT INTRODUCTIONS are for anyone wanting a stimulating and accessible way into a new subject. They are written by experts, and have been translated into more than 40 different languages.

The series began in 1995, and now covers a wide variety of topics in every discipline. The VSI library now contains over 350 volumes—a Very Short Introduction to everything from Psychology and Philosophy of Science to American History and Relativity—and continues to grow in every subject area.

Very Short Introductions available now:

Available soon:

For more information visit our website

www.oup.com/vsi/

Jaboury Ghazoul

FORESTS

A Very Short Introduction

OXFORD
UNIVERSITY PRESS

OXFORD

UNIVERSITY PRESS

Great Clarendon Street, Oxford, OX2 6DP,
United Kingdom

Oxford University Press is a department of the University of Oxford.
It furthers the University's objective of excellence in research, scholarship,
and education by publishing worldwide. Oxford is a registered trade mark of
Oxford University Press in the UK and in certain other countries

Published in the United States of America by Oxford University Press
198 Madison Avenue, New York, NY 10016, United States of America

British Library Cataloguing in Publication Data
Data available

Library of Congress Control Number: 2014959019

ISBN 978-0-19-870617-5

Printed and bound by
CPI Group (UK) Ltd, Croydon, CR0 4YY

To my parents, Ramez and Jemila, for their love.
To my parents-in-law, Wang and Kay, for
their tolerance.

Contents

Acknowledgements

The challenge of condensing our collected forest lore and
knowledge into a slim book could only be overcome by the
sedulous attention of Gnome (Katharine) Liston, my amazing wife,
who provided great ideas for points of entry into this vast field.
Yadvinder Malhi provided a useful critique of the manuscript, and
corrected some of my errors. The tree species richness table was
compiled with data kindly provided by David Allen, Mark Ashton,
Jennifer Baltzer, Min Cao, David Coomes, Alexandre de Oliveira,
Patrick Jansen, Jesse Kalwij, Gregory Gilbert, Kyle Harms, Dan
Johnson, Sue Laurance, Mike Lawes, Jim Lutz, William McShea,
Jonathan Myers, Vojtech Novotny, Becky Ostertag, Jan den Ouden,
Geoffrey Parker, Lawren Sack, and Sean Thomas. A great many
people (and too many to list) provided me with photos and images,
some of which I used, but most of which I could not include in this
short book. The images I did use were kindly provided by Rob
Marchant, Alicia Donnellan Barraclough, Jennifer Baltzer, Frank
Mannolini and Brad Seymour, Peter Crane, Andy MacGregor, Beat
Wermelinger, Edmond Dounias, Jakob Jäger, Patrice Levang, and
Robin Chazdon. Finally, thanks to Latha Menon for the
opportunity to write such a fun book.

List of illustrations

Forests

Chapter 1
Forests in human culture

The tree which moves some to tears of joy is, in the eyes of
others, only a green thing which stands in the way.

William Blake, 1799

On 10 December 1997, Julia 'Butterfly' Hill climbed a tall coastal
redwood tree in California (Figure 1). Two years and eight days
later she climbed back down again. Her two-year sojourn in the
canopy was to protest the logging of ancient forest trees by the
Pacific Lumber Company, and in doing so she became an unlikely
hero of a national and global movement to protect forests. Julia
Hill's stand against Pacific Lumber encapsulates two polarized
perceptions of forests, as resources ripe for exploitation or as
pristine Nature, venerable but vulnerable. Her protest is also
symbolic of the strong cultural and emotional values we, that is
society, attach to forests. It is difficult, by comparison, to imagine
anyone investing a similar commitment as Julia Hill to protest the
destruction of heathlands, peat bogs, or wild meadows, all of
which have suffered far greater proportionate losses than forests.

The furious public reaction against the proposed sale by the UK
government of around half of England's public forest estate in
2010 confirms that Julia Hill's remarkable protest is far from
fringe opinion. As the UK Environment Secretary Caroline
Spelman later commented, 'if there is one clear message from this

1. Julia 'Butterfly' Hill in a Californian coastal redwood tree, her home for two years.

experience, it is that people cherish their forests and woodlands and the benefits they bring' (17 February 2011). The emphasis is on the word 'cherish' which, far more than just the utilitarian values that forests provide, implies an affection and tenderness for forests that one might have for a friend or family member. Neither is non-violent action to protect forests confined to privileged Westerners. The Northern Indian Chipko movement has protected forests against indiscriminate exploitation for decades. In 1973 a confrontation over the cutting of trees was challenged by 'the matronly Gaura Devi [who] pushed herself forward, in front of the gun, and challenged the men to shoot her... She compared the forest with her mother's home.' The trees were not cut.

Forests, and particularly old growth forests, have long had a strong hold on the collective conscience of humankind, conjuring various interpretations, often more intuitive than factual. These include forests as benign life-supporting habitats of great biotic richness, or places invested with sacred worth and aesthetic beauty, or perhaps economically valuable resource-producing

2

lands, or even dangerous wastelands that are an impediment, even embarrassment, to human progress. In view of these different facets of forest identity it is no wonder that assessing the worth of forests has become a highly politicized and deeply divisive topic of public debate. Of all natural habitats, forests are among those that encompass the greatest and most deeply felt tensions. They are of considerable importance to the global community, to national economies, and to millions of people who traditionally depend on them directly, fully or partially, for their livelihoods. The value of forests to the international community as global carbon sinks or repositories of much of Earth's biodiversity also conflicts with national development priorities. For all these reasons, forests have become a focus of political debate. Moreover, the failure to acknowledge forests as, collectively, ecological entities, value-laden social concepts, and economically rewarding resources, has led to overly simplistic public, scientific, and management discourses that have done little to resolve forest management conflicts. While forests are ecological entities and land use units, we cannot separate ourselves entirely from a social frame of reference derived from our cultural and regional histories of forest exploitation and conservation. When we look at a forest we do not really see it as it is, but rather as we think it is.

A cultural history of forests

> I want to see Humbaba, god of the forest of whom people
> speak. I shall conquer Humbaba in the forest of Lebanese
> cedars. Then I shall cut down the cedars, to create a name
> for myself that shall last for all eternity.

Thus declared Gilgamesh, King of Uruk, as recounted in the *Epic of Gilgamesh*, dated to the New Sumerian Period around 2600 BC. Having duly killed the demon Humbaba, peace returned to the forest. But far from the forest being populated by evil monstrous beings, the *Epic of Gilgamesh* portrays the great cedar forest as a place of great beauty and comfort, and home to gods:

Gilgamesh and Enkidu froze and stared into the woods' great depth
and height. Then they were able to find and see the home of the
gods, the paradise of Ishtar's other self, called Imini-most-attractive.
All beauty true is ever there where gods do dwell, where there is cool
shade and harmony and sweet odoured food to match their mood.

These extracts from the oldest written tale convey the tension
that has characterized our relationship with forests throughout
human history to the present day. Gilgamesh and Enkidu
recognize the great cedar forest as a place of beauty and sanctity,
yet nevertheless go on to cut down the tallest trees. Humankind's
relationship with forests is long, complex, and contradictory.

Western cultural attitudes to forests have vacillated between
contrasting images of the natural and supernatural, places of
refuge and ambush, of purity and defilement, good and evil.
Forests have been feared as the abode of demons and dangers. Pan,
Lord of the Woods to the ancient Greeks, incurred *panic* in unwary
travellers. In medieval northern and central Europe forests were
home to trolls, sprites, dwarves, ogres, witches, werewolves, and
demons, which have survived to the modern day in *Hansel and
Gretel* and other fairy tales set in dark brooding forests. Quite apart
from any imagined dangers (which were probably real enough to
people at the time), forests had very real dangers in the form of
wild animals, notably bears and wolves, and outlaws and bandits.
The word 'wilderness', originally meaning 'place of wild beasts', is
virtually synonymous with forests, as indeed it is in its original
Nordic derivation. 'Weald' or 'woeld', Old English terms for forest,
are related to our modern 'wild'. The derivation of the word
'landscape' is also directly connected to woodland, and can be
traced back to roughly 500 AD to the Anglo-Saxon *landscaef*,
meaning a clearing in the *weald* with animals, huts, fields, and
fences. Landscape was, literally, carved out of the original forest.
The word 'forest' itself has had very different meanings throughout
history and only relatively recently has it been taken to mean a
tree-covered landscape (see Box 1).

Box 1 Forest semantics

Ambiguity about what was meant by 'forests' plagues our interpretation of woodland history in the Middle Ages. The nature of 'forest land' varied from country to country across Europe, and meanings change with time. The word 'forest' is derived from the Latin *foris*, meaning 'outside', and the related *forestare* meaning to 'keep out, place off limits, or exclude'. In Latin, a large tract of land covered with trees was instead referred to as a *sylva*, from whence the word silviculture is derived. Authorities of all kinds, be they kings, bishops, or nobles, were particularly interested in excluding the peasantry from certain lands, and hence around the time of Charlemagne in the 8th century 'forest' became a term referring to land placed off limits by royal decree, and had little direct relevance to tree cover.

Medieval Royal Forests were simply areas where the monarch enjoyed exclusive hunting rights. These lands contained villages, heaths, and cultivated lands, and often very few trees, examples in England being Exmoor and Sherwood Forest. Even as late as 1598 forest was described in John Manwood's *A Treatise and Discourse of the Lawes of the Forrest* as 'a certen territorie of wooddy grounds and fruitfull pastures, priviledged for wild beasts and foules of forrest, chase, and warren to rest and abide in, in the safe protection of the king, for his princely delight and pleasure'.

Not until the early to mid-19th century, with the development of scientific management practices of professional forestry in continental Europe, did it become the norm to equate forest with tree-covered land.

Forests have also been imbued with rather more positive supernatural and spiritual attributes, and superstitions and belief systems linked to trees and forests run deep in the histories of many diverse cultures (Figure 2). The fantastical creatures that

2. Tribal idols adorning a sacred forest site in Anamalai Wildlife Sanctuary, Western Ghats, India.

adorn Buddhist temples in Thailand, for example, represent the denizens of the mythical Himmapan forest through which, according to Buddhist tales, a traveller might pass from the earthly realm to heavenly planes. In the Holy Lands many adherents to Islam, Christianity, and Judaism, as well as the Druze (another monotheistic religion), continue to tie rags to trees as votive offerings or to pacify tree spirits despite proscriptions against the custom by religious establishments, a practice that is replicated in India and elsewhere. Throughout history it has been an almost universal feature of human society to ascribe ancestral souls to trees, and spirits to woods. To name but a few examples from very many, East African Wanika, Bornean Dayaks, and Buddhist animists took great care not to cut or damage old trees, which were accorded the respect appropriate to a venerated member of society. The Dieyerie tribe of South Australia, as well as many Philippine Islanders, Isan villagers in north-east Thailand, and many other cultures, used to regard sacred trees as being their transformed ancestors, or at least the homes of their ancestors, and avoided cutting them down. The *Kami* of Japanese Shinto refers to the sacred spirits or essence that are imbued in natural places, of which trees and forests are pre-eminent. In India, while forests were felled over the centuries, many small forest patches were retained within an agricultural matrix wherein various woodland spirits might find refuge. While similar beliefs have been gradually eroded among European societies, they are captured in literature. Shakespeare's forests, for example, are home to playful and mischievous fairies in *A Midsummer Night's Dream*, and the Forest of Arden of *As You Like It* is a peaceful refuge and sanctuary. More recently, in Tolkien's *Lord of the Rings* Fanghorn Forest counterpoints a brooding and menacing woodland with the ultimately benign ents.

For reasons of both fear and reverence, forests and trees were among the first places to be dedicated to gods. 'From the earliest times the worship of trees has played an important part in the religious life of European people', writes James George Frazer in

The Golden Bough (1894). Druidic cultures preceding the Roman occupation of Britain had strong spiritual and symbolic connections to woodland, particularly oak groves. Sacred forests inspired awe and fear. The Roman poet Lucan describes the sacred grove of Massilia (Marseille) as follows:

> A grove there was, untouched by men's hands from ancient times, whose interlacing boughs enclosed a space of darkness and cold shade, and banished the sunlight far above...Gods were worshipped there with savage rites, the altars were heaped with hideous offerings, and every tree was sprinkled with human gore. On those boughs birds feared to perch; in those coverts wild beasts would not lie down; no wind ever bore down on that wood, nor thunderbolt hurled down from the black clouds; the trees, even when they spread their leaves to no breeze, rustled of themselves...The people never resorted there to worship at close quarters, but left the place to the Gods.

On the other hand, European culture frequently likened forests to cathedrals or temples, reflecting a more benign sanctity. Indeed, it has been suggested that the pillars and vaulting structures of medieval cathedrals were designed to imitate the tall trunks and interlocking canopies of high forest.

While forests were both feared and sanctified, woodlands were also exploited. Forest products were essential for energy, raw materials, fruits and nuts, and forage for livestock (especially pigs), and therefore attitudes of fear or reverence were often ambivalent. The ancient Greeks considered forests to be humankind's original home (the first humans sprang from oak trees), but they still cut trees and cleared forests. The rise of Athens increased wood demand for building materials and energy, and for mining and shipbuilding, so much so that wood had to be imported from Macedonia and further afield. Plato, in his dialogue *Critias* (360 BC), discusses the effects of deforestation on soil erosion, the loss of animal habitats, and the impairment of water supplies. The outstanding administrative efficiency and engineering capacity of ancient Rome was no less effective at clearing forests, which were rapidly stripped from Roman lands. The Roman state gave title to anyone who cleared forest from land. Even Artemis (Roman Diana), goddess of forests and fertility, could not protect the oak forests which, even around the city of Ephesus where the Temple of Artemis stood, were quickly turned over to cultivated fields. The resulting soil erosion silted up the great harbour of Ephesus, forcing the city to relocate several times, and eventually caused its decline.

These contradictions between sanctity and utility persist today. Asian philosophies, as alluded to by Daoism, Buddhism, and Hinduism, have often been interpreted as harbouring more reverence for nature. Sacred forest groves in India and South East Asia owe their existence to such philosophies, as well as to animistic traditions that exist alongside them. The Buddha was never so happy as when meditating alone in the depths of a forest, and it is in the midst of a forest that he was shown the four great truths. Similarly, traditional African spiritual values and their blending with Christian beliefs have protected forests in Zimbabwe and Kenya. Yet sacred groves, be they in Africa, Asia, or elsewhere, are remnants of forest long since cleared. In recent decades even the groves themselves are exploited and cleared by the same communities that revere them, often being replaced by large shrines and temples or simply cut for their timber.

Neither are value systems static. Exposure to Western monotheistic religions, considered more anthropocentric and less sentimental of nature, has eroded some Asian beliefs that previously secured the protection of forests. Even so, there is little to indicate that non-Western religious creeds have been any better at protecting forests. Thus, while it has been popular to blame Judeo-Christian philosophies of the West for environmentally rapacious cultures that can only be invidiously compared to environmentally enlightened Asian, African, and indigenous American and Australian cultures, in truth people of all cultures have embarked on forest degradation to improve their comfort, security, and power according to circumstances. The impact of their actions has been affected as much by their technologies, the size of their populations, their power to subjugate others, and their beasts of burden, as by any particular cultural or religious environmentalism. The Maya, the Chinese, the Japanese, and the ancient Indus valley civilization all provide examples of early and extensive deforestation well before any European influence. In northern China neither Buddhism nor Confucianism were able to prevent the ascendency of development over conservation, and by the end of the T'ang dynasty (around 930 AD), large areas of forest had been denuded and transformed. Even demand for pine soot, required by the vast Chinese bureaucracy for ink, is implicated in the destruction of much of the pine forests of the T'ai-hang mountains between Shansi and Hopei. Similarly, Japanese Shinto's reverence for natural places often took second place to the needs of an expanding and increasingly affluent population following the eventual closure of the chaotic and lawless *Sengoku jidai* (the Japanese 'warring states period') at the end of the 16th century. By the end of the 17th century monumental building projects, made possible by the outbreak of peace, had devastated many of Japan's forests. More recently, opportunities afforded by the expansion of free market economies have undercut taboos. Spirits and ancestors can be appeased or removed from areas that developers wish to exploit. In Indonesia, the common Javanese term for development, *babad alas*, literally means to open up or clear forest, but villagers often circumvent religious proscriptions by preceding the clearance of forest (or harvesting of ironwood, camphor, or other valuable trees) with rites and offerings to propitiate the forest or tree spirits.

The conception of forests as wild areas to be tamed and exploited by felling, fire, and farming has nonetheless been particularly prevalent in Europe, from Classical times to the post-medieval period. This view was explicit in the ideological and actual destruction by the new Christian order of sacred groves and trees long venerated by pagan societies in the Middle Ages, as typified by the destruction of Donar's Oak by St Boniface in 8th-century Germany. European expansion exported such ideas to other parts of the world, and particularly to North America where forest clearance and the establishment of a new agrarian order was re-enacted from the 17th century. In Europe and North America this process drew inspiration from Christian concepts of morality, the hard work of humble pioneers being represented as a struggle against a wild, uncivilized, and unyielding nature. This sacred motive came to have an increasingly secular utilitarian counterpart, which held that progress and development are necessary for civilization and survival. Forest clearance and development delivered both moral and material rewards.

Historical descriptions of forests can be misleading if we ignore the underlying motives and perspectives of the writers. Early explorers of the New World were keen to advertise the economic potential of their newly discovered regions and to justify the purpose of their expeditions, and so often talked of forests in glowing terms. Despite venturing no further than the coast, the Florentine explorer Giovanni da Verrazzano, the first European to visit the North American Atlantic coast since the Norse, reported 'a land full of the largest forests, some thin and some dense, clothed with various sorts of trees, with as much beauty and delectable appearance as it would be possible to express'. Settlers thought differently. The Pilgrim William Bradford wrote of New England as 'hideous and desolate', his description being shaped by the hard labour necessary to clear forests to establish his embryonic colony.

The Romantic period: a change of attitude

The Judeo-Christian interpretation of nature as being provided by God for the benefit of, and exploitation by, humankind began to be challenged by the English botanist John Ray (1627–1705). In *The Wisdom of God Manifested in the Works of Creation* (1691) he argued that 'it is generally received opinion that all this visible world was created for Man ... as if there were no other end of any creature but some way or other to be serviceable to man, ... yet wise men nowadays think otherwise'. The idea of rights of existence independent of any utilitarian value to humans, as portrayed by John Ray, was reiterated by others. Alexander Pope (1688–1744) in his *Essay on Man* (1733) wrote that living things 'Are all but parts of one stupendous whole, Whose body Nature is, and God the soul'. In *A Philosophical Survey of the Animal Creation* (1768) John Bruckner (1726–1804) expressed concern that the English transformation of American forests might break the 'web of life'. Meanwhile, the doctrine of the 'Sublime' revelled in a new appreciation of the visceral and terrible beauty of natural landscapes (Figure 3). Edmund Burke's (1729–97) *A Philosophical Enquiry into the Origins of Our Ideas of the Sublime and Beautiful* equated beauty with ordered and safe representations, but the sublime was derived from visions that invoked a mix of awe and terror that is 'productive of the strongest emotion which the mind is capable of feeling'. Forests were still dark and foreboding, but were now appreciated all the more for that.

European sentiments towards forests, and nature more generally, changed more dramatically at the end of the 18th century with the Romantic movement's reaction to the Enlightenment, and particularly to industrialization and the scientific rationalization on which it was based. A respect for wild nature took centre stage and was associated with innocence, beauty, and spiritual and mental health, as reflected in the Romantic painting and literature of the 18th and early 19th centuries. The attitudinal shift was also facilitated, paradoxically, by the Enlightenment, which interpreted

3. *Kindred Spirits* (1849), an iconic painting by Asher Brand Durand of American landscape art, expressing a sense of the sublime wilderness.

the workings of Nature through the prism of scientific advancement as the expression of God's splendour. The new appreciation of forests and forested landscapes became reflected in literature and art in the late 18th century and was extolled by, among many others, William Wordsworth in England and William Cullen Bryant in North America. François-René de Chateaubriand, inspired by the forested landscapes of North

America, prompted the development of Romantic ideals in France. Nonetheless, while the Romantic period represented a marked shift in attitude to forests and nature, industrialization and rural development continued, and concepts of pioneering progress on both sides of the Atlantic remained strong.

Emergence of modern attitudes

It is in central Europe that modern concepts of forest management were established, but in North America that Western concepts of forests as vestiges of wild nature needing protection were born. The denuded Mediterranean basin impressed George Perkins Marsh (1801–82) of the need to conserve forests for future resource security, a concept that he took back to his native America and promoted in his great book *Man and Nature*. Such views were not new, being preceded by Michaux's three-volume *North American Sylva* (1817), though their adoption was slow. Nonetheless, they shaped the views of Gifford Pinchot (1865–1946) who advocated sustainable management of resources and railed against the dominant American myth that resources were inexhaustible. It was the combination of Pinchot's leadership and the enthusiastic support of President Theodore Roosevelt that stimulated a surge of conservation-oriented forest management after 1900.

Meanwhile, a more aesthetic and emotional response to forests was being developed through the writings of Henry David Thoreau (1817–62), who valued forests as part of a 'partially cultivated country', which reflects many modern conceptions of nature conservation. John Muir (1838–1914) placed more emphasis on the inherent value of wilderness, and devoted his life to the preservation of forests in the western United States. Aldo Leopold's (1887–1948) 'land ethic' viewed humans as citizens of the 'land community' ('ecosystem' in current terminology) rather than conquerors of it. Leopold accepted the need to use and manage the land, but also recognized that forests and their denizens were legitimate and necessary elements of a healthy landscape. Leopold's writings became particularly influential after the impetus provided by Rachel Carson's *Silent Spring* (1962), whose central concept was nature as 'a single intricate web of life'.

In Europe, lacking North America's wilderness areas and with many more people, chronic timber famines and the need for wood production on a sustained basis forced the development of scientific forest management in 19th-century Germany, building on foundations established in the 18th century (e.g. the *Schlagwaldwirtschaft* system of forest management). Advancing the science of forest management was one thing; getting German land owners to change their patterns of mismanagement was another. Nonetheless, schools of forestry were established in France and Germany during the mid-1800s. During the late 19th and early 20th centuries, the scientific practice of forestry spread through all of Europe and its colonies (the Imperial Forest Research Institute being established in 1906 in Dehradun in British India), and influenced forest management in the United States.

Clash of cultures

European scientific forestry practices were founded on the need to conserve forests for the production of timber and other resources, and on the preconception that increased demands for forest resources, particularly since the late 19th century, would lead to widespread forest loss and degradation if unchecked. These ideas were transferred and applied to the tropics. Forests were brought under state control, notwithstanding traditional forms of land ownership and practice that were either not recognized or ignored by colonial administrations. European narratives of forest change often equated the supposed original forest cover as being equivalent to the area that was deemed capable of supporting forests under current biophysical conditions. Any departure from this was taken to represent deforestation by human agency, and presumed mismanagement by local people. Naturally, this justified the transfer of forests to state control. This narrative, which continues to hold much weight in the forest science and conservation community, ignored the validity of traditional land management systems that, far from causing forest degradation and clearance, have served to maintain and, in some cases, even increase forest cover.

This has been particularly so in the tropics, where shifting cultivators often bore the brunt of the blame for tropical deforestation. Shifting cultivators are subsistence farmers who clear and burn patches of forests which they then crop for a few years, after which the land is left fallow to regenerate. These people have probably never exceeded more than a few tens of millions worldwide, around 1 per cent of the world's population, yet reported estimates of their share of tropical deforestation reach as high as 60 per cent. In reality, deforestation in the past century has been driven by several factors. Shifting cultivation is undoubtedly one of the more visible causes, but it is overshadowed by cattle ranching and agricultural development, unregulated logging, economic development projects, road building, and mining. Yet the emphasis on shifting cultivation coupled with population growth was, until recently, entrenched in Western explanations of forest destruction. This is exemplified by a World Bank report on deforestation in West and Central Africa, which argued that although shifting cultivation was sustainable at low population densities, 'with the shock of extremely rapid population growth...these practices could not evolve fast enough. Thus they became the major source of forest destruction and degradation of the rural environment'.

This view is now challenged. Shifting cultivation, rather than being wasteful and destructive, is more often a sustainable and sophisticated land use system that maximizes resource use efficiencies while minimizing risks. Changing socio-economic conditions, growing populations, and reduced land availability have led to a shortening of fallow periods and less time for forest recovery. On this basis land use degradation and forest collapse has been predicted, but evidence for such collapse, even with short fallow periods, is not generally evident. The reason that shifting cultivation has been conceptualized as a deforestation problem (rather than a sustainable management system) lies in the failure of Western science to understand the long history of traditional forest cultivation systems and the knowledge on which they are based.

Forest cover in West Africa, the subject of the World Bank report, has in fact fluctuated over historical times due to changing human activities and climatic changes. Far from attributing deforestation to recent population expansion and poor land management, there is substantial anthropological evidence showing that people in the forest-savannah zone of West Africa actively *created* forest patches around settlements, and were instrumental in transforming non-wooded savannah to a mosaic of forest patches set within a grassland matrix. Traditional management served to protect and even enhance forests. Hunters set early and mid-season fires that provided protection from more devastating fires later in the season. Home gardens planted with favoured trees initiated and enriched forest islands around settlements. Village rules protected trees and imposed schedules for cattle grazing and fallow rotations which prevented overgrazing. Expanded agricultural activities had not necessarily led to wholesale degradation of forest cover, as often purported. This is not to say that communities in Africa are innocent of deforestation, but rather that processes of land cover change are more complex than Western perceptions might envisage.

The expansion of intensive agriculture and plantation forestry since the 1950s is but the latest phase of a long history of natural forest loss. Contemporary deforestation in terms of area of lost natural forest is, however, primarily a tropical affair spanning decades. It can be largely attributed to agricultural expansion by industrial enterprises responding to global market demands.

Continued growth of the global human population, coupled with our increasing wealth, maintains high demand for agricultural products (and particularly meat that requires extensive pasture lands), as well as other resources derived from forested areas such as timber and minerals. Although forests have long been an important component of landscapes throughout human history, unprecedented demographic pressures are beginning to create novel landscapes where forests are all but excluded.

Current conflicts, future concerns

Today, society's conflicted forest values remain, and both conservation and clearance of tropical forests continue apace. As a generalization, forest continues to be cleared in the tropics but appears to be expanding once more in temperate zones. The need to feed our rapidly growing world population is at the expense of forests cleared for agriculture. Growing world markets demand more timber and a diverse array of other products that forest industries supply, often from sustainably managed sources, but often not.

It has recently become fashionable to emphasize that forests supply humanity with a wide array of environmental benefits, a concept encapsulated as forest 'ecosystem services'. These services, if financially valued and internalized within accounting systems, can, it is argued, justify the conservation of tracts of forests on economic grounds. Julia Hill, on the other hand, represents a school of thought that emphasizes humanity's innate affinity for the natural world. This view, popularized as 'biophilia' by Edward Wilson, presents the natural world, of which forests are a principal component and potent symbol, as integral to our development as individuals. Conversely, the loss of forests, or our estrangement from them through our increasingly urbanized and technologically based lifestyles, implies serious consequences for individual psychology and societal well-being.

There is no single cultural conception of forests. In all cultures attitudes to forests are conflicting and contradictory, encompassing feelings that range from revulsion and fear to purity and spiritual profundity. Yet humans have long depended on forests for resources, though the scale of exploitation has been sufficient to motivate Julia Hill and others like her to go to extraordinary lengths to preserve what are perceived to be primeval, old growth, and natural forest. Whether we favour the urban jungle or the rural rides, forests remain very much part of our economy and culture. In recent decades, we have come to realize that they are also an essential part of our future. Our natural resources, Earth's biodiversity, and the global climate depend, in large part, on the security of global forests. Yet the centrality of forests in our collective cultural and spiritual histories suggests that our losses will be far more than just economic.

Chapter 2
Many forests

Defining forests

Conceptions of what forests are, and how they are defined, vary depending on who is doing the defining. Foresters, ecologists, or farmers (or for that matter, lawyers, urban planners, or furniture makers) might have very different concepts of forests, as might the people of Great Britain or France compared to those of Brazil or Pakistan. Different environmental and cultural histories affect peoples' visions of what forests are. It is perhaps not surprising, therefore, that as many as 800 different definitions of forests and woodland areas have been collated from around the world. Indeed, the many different purposes that people use forests for, and the many varieties of forest types, justifies many definitions, each suited to a particular social perception and bioclimatic region.

Why then concern ourselves with a single definition of forest when there are many locally appropriate definitions? One reason is that definitions have national and global policy implications. The Kyoto Protocol on climate change called for, among other things, the reporting on greenhouse gas emissions resulting 'from direct human-induced land use change and forestry activities, limited to afforestation, reforestation and deforestation since 1990'. This becomes a problem when forest definitions (and hence the meanings of afforestation, reforestation, and deforestation) vary from one country to another. If we cannot account for these differences then we can place little faith in global forestry statistics.

In its simplest and broadest sense, a forest is 'an area that is covered by trees'. To most of us trees are single-stemmed woody perennial plants. Yet some national definitions of 'tree' also encompass palms, tree ferns, bamboos, vines, stumps, coppice shoots, and many other plant forms. Indeed, across the world's nations there are more than sixty legally recognized definitions of 'tree'. Bamboo is a grass in most countries, but a tree in much of East Asia (Figure 4). In semi-arid countries even shrubs and bushes, as the most common woody vegetation, might be elevated to tree status. For the sake of simplicity, let's accept that trees are, in the strict sense, self-supported single-stemmed woody plants. This excludes palms, tree ferns, and bamboos which have fibrous (non-woody) stems, and vines which are not self-supporting.

Our next difficulty in defining forests is to clarify what we mean by 'an area covered by trees'. This may be an administrative unit, a type of land use, or a type of land cover. Least interesting, and least useful, is forest as an administrative unit, in which case a forest is an area of land classified as such under legal ordinance, regardless of whether it has trees or not. National forest lands fall under this category.

Definitions based on land use emphasize utilitarian values of forests. The United States Northwest Regional Environment Office, for example, defines forest as 'land, other than land owned by the federal government, that was available for and capable of growing a crop of trees of any commercial species used to produce lumber and other forest products, including Christmas trees'. This refers to timber production, but different utilitarian definitions might also include other forest products, recreation, or even

4. Bamboo in Japan. This is a forest in East Asia, but not a forest anywhere else.

protection. The Chinese Ministry of Forestry includes windbreaks and some fruit orchards in its forest statistics, while South Korea specifically excludes orchards.

The interpretation of forest as a type of land cover is also fraught with ambiguity. We might think of forests as large, densely wooded regions in remote areas with few people, but this leaves open to interpretation what is meant by large, dense, remote, and few. Land cover definitions often refer to a minimum extent of canopy cover, but this can vary from as little as 1 per cent to over 80 per cent (see Table 1). A change in the threshold canopy cover can dramatically change reported forest extent. In 2000 the UN Food and Agriculture Organization (FAO) changed its definition of 'forest' in developed countries from 20 per cent tree cover to 10 per cent cover to harmonize with the definition applied to developing countries. At the stroke of a pen this increased recorded forest cover in Australia from 40,000 to 158,000 square kilometres.

Other ecologically focused definitions emphasize the sense of forest as a community of interacting organisms, but still retain readily measureable criteria. Thus British Columbia's Ministry of Forests and Range expresses forests as 'a complex community of plants and animals in which trees are the most conspicuous members and where the tree crown density is greater than 10 percent'.

Table 1 Range of thresholds to define forests used by various nations

Criterion	Lowest threshold	Highest threshold
Forest area (ha)	0.01 (Belgium)	100 (Malawi, Papua New Guinea)
Canopy cover (%)	1 (Iran)	80 (Malawi, Zimbabwe)
Tree height (m)	1.3 (Estonia)	15 (Zimbabwe)

In short, no single definition satisfies all interpretations and purposes, and the diversity of definitions might simply reflect the great variety of forest types that exist. Even so, it remains necessary to have a widely accepted working definition. In this respect the somewhat unwieldy but widely accepted FAO definition, encompassing both land cover and land use interpretations, is as good as any (see Box 2). Based on this definition, forests cover around forty-two million square kilometres in tropical, temperate, and boreal lands, or approximately 30 per cent of the global land surface.

Forests are not simply collections of trees, as many definitions might imply. Forests are ecosystems that encompass lakes, rivers, grasslands, marshlands, peatlands, and other habitats. Apart from supporting a diverse array of forest wildlife, the different habitats of forested ecosystems are intimately connected to each other through flows of energy and nutrients. In the boreal forests of North America's Pacific coast, for example, tree growth rates are

Box 2 UN Food and Agriculture Organization definition of 'forest'

Forest: land with tree crown cover (or equivalent stocking level) of more than 10 per cent and area of more than 0.5 hectares. The trees should be able to reach a minimum height of five metres at maturity *in situ*. May consist either of closed forest formations where trees of various storeys and undergrowth cover a high proportion of the ground; or open forest formations with a continuous vegetation cover in which tree crown cover exceeds 10 per cent. Young natural stands and all plantations established for forestry purposes which have yet to reach a crown density of 10 per cent or tree height of five metres are included under forest, as are areas normally forming part of the forest area which are temporarily unstocked as a result of human intervention or natural causes but which are expected to revert to forest.

often much higher close to rivers. Trees in these riparian zones might derive as much as 24 per cent of their nitrogen requirements from rivers. This fertilization effect is facilitated by salmon which, having spent most of their lives feeding and growing at sea, return in their thousands to spawn and die in their natal streams deep in the boreal forests. Salmon carcasses, and thus the marine nutrients from which they are built, are distributed into the forest by flooding and by animals that scatter faeces, urine, and partially eaten carcasses. Herbivorous insects feeding on nutrient enriched leaves become more abundant. The transfer of energy continues up through the food web. The densities of golden-crowned kinglet and other forest birds that feed on insects can be linked to the biomass of salmon in local streams.

The distribution, composition, and dynamics of forests can be broadly understood on the basis of climate and soil. Precipitation and temperature alone are sufficient to provide a useful framework for sorting the world's terrestrial biomes into recognizably distinct categories (Figure 5). Of course, this simple climatic template obscures many local and regional variations in forest type and composition, including the role of evolutionary and biogeographical histories, topography (which modifies local climate and affects drainage), and soil (reflecting the combined effect of geology, climate, and biology).

Thus different regions with equivalent climates can support forests that might differ markedly in physiognomy and composition. The temperate rainforests of America's Pacific Northwest are, for example, dominated by conifers, while broadleaved trees are far more abundant in temperate rainforests of the southern hemisphere (e.g. New Zealand and South America). Nonetheless, they can still be recognized as belonging to the same climatically determined forest type. That similar forest types readily map on to a typology determined by only two climatic variables emphasizes the importance of these variables in

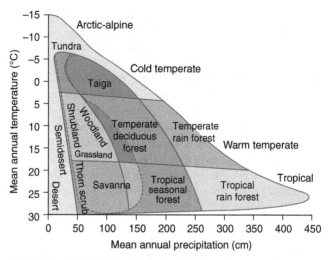

5. Whittaker's distribution of biomes in relation to temperature and precipitation.

shaping forest structure. Climate therefore provides a fundamental starting point for understanding the world's vegetation.

We can explore the main forest biomes by taking a metaphorical trip, starting in Africa's equatorial tropical forests and working our way north till we reach the fringes of the Arctic tundra. From time to time we will take a detour, or a continental leap, to explore variations on a theme.

Tropical rainforests

We begin in the tropical rainforests of the Congo Basin where the climate is permanently warm, wet, and frost-free. Indeed, today it is hot and humid, but in the forest understorey the shade provides respite from the heat. The forest trees are tall, the canopy is perhaps some forty or fifty metres above us, and they are evergreen and broadleaved—there are no conifers here. All look roughly similar in structure and form, but there are enough subtle differences to indicate that each is different, and that there are many kinds. The trunks of the biggest trees easily exceed a metre in diameter, and some are supported by immense buttresses that provide stability (Figure 6). Long-stemmed woody vines, or lianas (Figure 7), reach from the ground to the canopy, sometimes weaving through several tree crowns. Many large tree branches are laden with ferns and orchids (Figure 8). There are many birds, but they are high up and difficult to see. Primates and other mammals are also moving through the canopy, but they too are more often heard than seen. There are many insects, the mosquitoes are particularly vicious, but at least we avoid the leeches that would have plagued us in South East Asia's wet forests.

The forest understorey we walk through is dark, as the dense canopy has filtered out most of the sunlight. Occasional gaps in the canopy have been formed by fallen branches or trees, and here light floods the forest floor which is now covered with a profusion of herbs and saplings that grow all around the rapidly decaying fallen branches. There are many butterflies in these forest gaps, and bees too. Ants are everywhere. We are attracted by a sweet smell nearby which we find to be rotting fruit lying on the forest floor, clearly fallen or dropped from the tree above. Ants, butterflies, and other insects are lapping up the juice, but small sharp teeth marks in the flesh of the fruit suggest these husks are just the remains of someone else's feast. Much of what we see on the forest floor seems to be in a state of decay, and fungi of many different forms and colours abound. It rains again, and we take shelter under the thickness of the leafy canopy, but we get wet all the same. The rain comes down hard and fast, and runs down the tree stems as innumerable small streams. Eventually the storm passes, and water vapour rises thickly from the ground.

Had we started our walk in Borneo our experience would have been broadly similar, although the trees would be taller, with the

6. Buttresses on a spurwood tree (*Dysoxylum pettigrewianum*) at Mossman Gorge, Australian Wet Tropics.

7. Woody vines, or lianas, scrambling up towards the canopy in tropical rainforest in Sabah, Borneo.

8. An epiphytic orchid, *Agrostophyllum majus*, on a tree trunk in Bornean rainforest.

canopy some fifty to sixty metres in height, and some especially tall trees rising above the canopy to eighty metres (Figure 9). Indeed, the archetypal tropical rainforests of most people's imaginations might be these lofty Bornean forests. The diversity of trees is even richer than that of the Congo, though a botanist would tell us that most of the canopy trees belong to just a single, though highly diverse, tree family, the Dipterocarpaceae.

Back in the Congo, we continue walking north until we come across, relatively abruptly, forest where the trees all look very similar. The climate is much the same as it was before (we have not walked far) but almost all the trees in this tropical rainforest belong to a single species. This is odd and belies our assumptions that tropical rainforests are rich and diverse, as this forest is clearly not. We are in the Ituri Forest of north-eastern Congo where a single species *Gilbertiodendron dewevrei* (known locally as limbali) accounts for 80 per cent of canopy trees. The understorey here is particularly dark under the dense shade of the limbali trees, and the leaf litter under our feet is much thicker than before. It seems that few seedlings of any species other than limbali are able to establish in these conditions.

In Borneo we might have come across forest on peat soils similarly dominated by a single species, *Shorea albida* (balau), one of the dipterocarps. Elsewhere in Borneo we might pass through low but dense heath forest on nutrient poor sandy soils where the canopy barely attains fifteen metres. On an Amazon forest walk we would have been similarly confused by the many different tree species, but here too we might come across forest understories packed with little other than palms, or strayed into the forests of the Rio Negro basin where all is quiet, insects and animals are few and mosquitoes, thankfully, are absent.

As we prepare to leave the ever-wet equatorial rainforest zone, we reflect that there are many tropical rainforests. Some are highly diverse and rich in tree and animal species, while others have but

9. A tall *Koompassia excelsa* tree from tropical rainforest in Sabah, Borneo.

few tree species and are monotonous by comparison. There are regional differences too. Dipterocarp trees dominate the Asian rainforests but are almost absent in the American tropics. Local variation in forest types has much to do with local weather patterns, soil and geological conditions, and altitudinal and latitudinal position, while regional differences among continents need to be traced to tectonic and evolutionary histories that take us back millions of years.

Tropical montane cloud forest

As we skirt round the eastern edge of the Congo Basin we climb a series of terraces which takes us through densely cultivated areas. The lush growth attests to the fertility of the soils in this region. We climb further, over difficult terrain, and are rewarded by the prospect of cool misty montane forest. Here the trees are gnarled, small, and closely set. Leaves are much smaller than those of lowland trees, and they lack the elongated leaf tips that shed excessive water after a lowland tropical downpour. The atmosphere is laden with water, but there is little rain. The canopy lies but a few metres above our heads, but ever-present mist obscures colours. A hanging garden of epiphytes—plants that grow on other plants—is draped over every tree branch, but the large buttressed trees and lianas of the lowlands are gone.

It is beautiful, almost mystical forest, but our delight with the surroundings is tempered by steep and slippery slopes and twisted densely set stems that impede our progress. Peering through the mist to gauge a way through we decide that the best course of action is to take a short break. As we do we ponder on the mist that is as much fantastical as it is frustrating. Water evaporated off the sea or from the lowland forest below has been carried by warm air currents to the mountain. Here the humid air has been forced to rise up the mountainside where it cools. As the water vapour condenses it forms the water droplets that appear as clouds and mist.

It is the epiphytic communities, the thick wet mats of ferns, orchids, and, in the American tropics, bromeliads that cover tree branches wherever we look, that most impresses us. Almost 200 species of orchids, ferns, and bromeliads have been found perched in the crown of single strangler fig tree in Peruvian montane cloud forest. Similar richness is found in Asian cloud forests, although there are no bromeliads here. These mats are home to a myriad of invertebrates that dwell within the accumulated detritus and humus that has collected over the decades. On these subsist a plethora of amphibians that are particularly at home in the ever-moist conditions.

Montane forests are often isolated from one another by expanses of intervening warmer lowland areas. This geographic and thermal isolation has facilitated separate evolutionary trajectories. Consequently, a disproportionate number of montane forest species are endemic, often being found nowhere on Earth other than a single mountain. Africa's Eastern Arc montane forests, for example, are home to around 2,000 plant species of which 800 are endemic, and up to 80 per cent of the invertebrates can be unique to single montane forest in this area. Although cold, wet, and exhausted, our time in the montane cloud forests has been highly rewarding.

Tropical seasonal forest

We tend to think of tropical rainforests as being permanently wet, but in fact it is only the equatorial forests that are wet all year round (and even then some are not). Further from the equator we move into the seasonally wet forest zones. Annual rainfall is lower than in the equatorial zone and there is an increasingly long dry period. This dry season, in which monthly rainfall is less than 100 mm, can last several months. Seasonally wet forests are often as lofty as non-seasonal tropical forests, and are similar in structure. Deciduous trees are more common on account of periods of annual water stress. Branches are festooned with orchids and ferns. In the Neotropics bromeliads cover the tree branches. Apart from a few months of comparatively dry weather, there is little to distinguish seasonal rainforests from those on the equator, and one type grades into the other with no obvious distinction. Seasonal forests are the most extensive rainforest formations. They cover much of Central America, Brazil's Atlantic forests, and south-eastern Amazon. They also occur on the margins of the main rainforest blocks in South East Asia and the monsoon systems of India's Western Ghats and Australia's wet tropics. Most of the African wet tropics are distinctly seasonal, although the dry seasons are less predictable than elsewhere.

Tropical dry forest and savannah woodlands

Moving further north rainfall continues to decline, and the duration and intensity of the annual dry period increases. We begin to enter more deciduous open forests, though the change is gradual. When the seasonal dry period regularly lasts six months or more forests are commonly known as 'tropical dry forests' (Figure 10). These are less floristically rich than rainforests, but could still include several hundred plant species in any local area.

On the other hand, they can also be very species poor. Had we been travelling south from the equator rather than north we would have come across mopane forests, almost entirely dominated by the mopane tree (*Colophospermum mopane*), although the richer miombo woodlands form the most extensive warm dry forest type in southern Africa. Miombo is a common local name for various species of *Brachystegia* that are the woodland's most characteristic species. Miombo woodland occurs from the Atlantic coast in Angola, across Zambia, Malawi, much of Zimbabwe, and almost to the east African coast in Mozambique and Tanzania. There is surprisingly little variation in this forest type across its huge range, with species of *Brachystegia* and two other genera, *Julbernardia* and *Isoberlinia*, dominating throughout.

10. Madagascar's Spiny Forest, a dry deciduous forest that includes trees, such as the baobab (*Adansonia rubrostipa*), that are adapted to conserve and store water.

Back in the northern hemisphere, we are now in a narrow band of dry forest that extends from the Atlantic coast of western Africa east across the southern fringes of the Sahara Desert to the Ethiopian Highlands and Red Sea coast. The forest is patchy, having been extensively modified by human activities such as cultivation and burning. Much of the woodland is of secondary origin having recovered after previous episodes of clearance, and it is difficult to determine natural forest formations. Nonetheless, there are obvious differences to the wetter forests we left behind. There are no lianas, nor are there any orchids or ferns to adorn the tree branches. The stature of the forest is also much shorter, achieving little more than twenty metres in height. Trees are widely spaced and plenty of light filters into the understorey.

Here too there are regional differences shaped by variation in climate, soil, and evolutionary histories. To the west broadleaved trees are common, but further east the dry forests are instead dominated by fine-leaved species, notably acacias. Had we been in the Australian outback we would also have encountered many acacias (*Acacia*), although here eucalypt trees (mainly *Eucalyptus*, *Corymbia*, and *Angophora*) and banksias (*Banksia*) would provide these forests with a uniquely Australian feel (Figure 11). Asian dry forests are again dominated by several species of that classically tropical Asian family, the dipterocarps.

With increasing water scarcity grasses become more abundant, and we move from dry forests to savannah woodlands where canopy cover might be as low as 20 per cent. Tree cover in this zone is adapted to drought and fire. These dry savannah forests occur widely in South America where they are known as *cerrado* (savannahs), *chaco* (dry woodlands), or *caatinga* (arid thorny scrub forest). They are similarly extensive north, south, and east of the Congo Basin in Africa, in southern Madagascar, and in much of India and continental South East Asia. Most of Australia's woodland cover also belongs to this category.

Mediterranean woodlands

Having crossed the Sahara desert we finally reach the woodlands of the Mediterranean coast and its hinterland. Hot

11. Dry savannah forests near Chillagoe, Queensland, Australia, comprising many *Acacia* and *Banksia* trees.

dry summers are offset by wetter mild winters that allow trees to establish. Short evergreen shrubs are overtopped by evergreen oaks or olive trees that have thick, leathery leaves to retain water when it's hot. A variety of soils and climates in the hills of northern Morocco, Algeria, and Tunisia, and across the Straits of Gibraltar into Spain, support a diverse mix of holm and cork oak (*Quercus ilex* and *Q. suber*) woodlands, wild olive (*Olea oleaster*), and carob (*Ceratonia siliqua*) woodlands and, in the milder lowlands, Berber thuya (*Tetraclinis articulata*) forests. The holm oak, which cannot tolerate frosts, is becoming increasingly familiar in northern Europe as climate change facilitates its spread. At higher elevations in the Atlas Mountains of Morocco and Algeria extensive stands of magnificent but now endangered Atlas cedar (*Cedrus atlantica*) provide a home for the equally endangered Barbary macaques, while cork oak woodlands on the Iberian peninsula are home to the critically endangered Iberian lynx.

Temperate deciduous forests

As we descend the northern slopes of the Alps into the European temperate zone, with the lingering memory of the rich tropical forests, the deciduous forests we now encounter will prove somewhat disappointing in the richness of tree species. These forests appear to have little more than ten different types of tree in any one place. But if we take the time to look down and around us we will find that there are a great many different plant species among the understorey herbs of the forest floor. Indeed, around 90 per cent of the plant richness of temperate deciduous forests is found in the herbaceous understorey. Gone too is the profusion of woody lianas of the tropics, and tree branches host little more than some lichens and occasional small ferns.

If we could linger awhile, we would notice a distinctive feature of these forests: they are strongly seasonal, with a winter dormant period when most trees lose their leaves and grow little, if at all. Most of these deciduous trees are oak, beech (*Fagus*), birch (*Betula*), hornbeam (*Carpinus*), ash (*Fraxinus*), maple (*Acer*), chestnut (*Castanea*), and lime (*Tilia*). In upland areas these deciduous trees give way to evergreen conifers (Figure 12). As in the tropics, there is no single temperate forest type. Variation in geology, soil, topography, and exposure, coupled with the long history of human land use, conspire to give us many different forest constellations.

Had our walk taken us through the temperate deciduous forests of eastern North America or Japan our experience would have been superficially similar. These regions share many of the same types of tree as Europe. Although there are more species in eastern North American and East Asian woodlands, we would nevertheless have recognized aspens (*Populus*), birches, maples, elms (*Ulmus*), oaks, and beeches in North America, and in Japan oak, elm, lime, ash, and maple would similarly have provided a familiar forest setting.

12. Deciduous beech forest in the low Alps in Ticino, Switzerland, with evergreen conifer forest in the distance.

We will not fail to notice that the European temperate forests have been shaped by human management. The history of management is writ in the structure and composition of the woodlands, but the language can be cryptic and difficult to decipher. Nonetheless, one unmistakable feature is the abundance of multi-stemmed trees. Many hardwood species, in contrast to their tropical or coniferous counterparts, readily sprout multiple new shoots from roots and stumps following stem cutting. This phenomenon is the basis for coppice forestry, long used in Europe to provide uniformly sized poles for fuelwood, fencing, and construction.

Temperate rainforest

Moving a little further north through Britain and up to the northwest highlands of Scotland we begin to encounter in sheltered coastal inlets and glens small patches of a rather more distinctive forest type. Epiphytes—which we last encountered in abundance in the seasonal tropics—are back, although they are now represented by mosses, liverworts, and lichens on oak trees. The luxuriant growth on these trees benefits from very high rainfall coming in off the Atlantic Ocean on the prevailing westerly winds. It rains a lot here, and even when it is not raining there is a thick mist hanging over the understorey.

In truth, these small patches of temperate rainforest in isolated glens of the Scottish west coast do not do justice to this forest formation, which is instead much better represented in the Pacific Northwest of America, where conifers such as Douglas fir (*Pseudotsuga menziesii*), western hemlocks (*Tsuga heterophylla*), Sitka spruce (*Picea sitchensis*), and western red cedar (*Thuja plicata*) attain immense height and bulk. High winter rainfall coupled with summer fogs keep the forests wet throughout the year. Mosses and lichens are very common, sustained by the high rainfall and humidity which alleviates water stress on these plants that lack roots. Carpets of these epiphytes are draped over and completely obscure large tree branches.

In the southern hemisphere the much higher sea to land ratio has created excellent conditions for extensive temperate rainforests on the west coasts of Chile and New Zealand. It is very wet as we push our way through the dense and sodden vegetation, and epiphytes are again common. Here, however, the trees are less familiar to northern sensibilities, and comprise southern taxa such as southern beech (*Nothofagus*) and conifers of the Araucariaceae (monkey puzzle trees) and Podocarpaceae—as familiar to residents of the southern hemisphere as oaks and beeches are to those in the northern hemisphere. In Chile these forests might be overtopped by impressively tall alerce trees (*Fitzroya cupressoides*) that might attain seventy metres in height, while in all these regions tree ferns are common in the understorey. The distribution of southern beeches, podocarps, araucarias, and tree ferns across southern South America, Australia, and New Zealand, together with the discovery of *Fitzroya* fossils in Tasmania, is a legacy of the once continuous forests that existed across the ancient continent of Gondwana from which these land masses fragmented from around 180 million years ago.

Boreal forests

Returning to Europe we catch a boat from northern Scotland across to Scandinavia and make our way across to Finland and northern Russia. We are in the boreal forest, also known as taiga, a vast area that extends across the northern hemisphere from Alaska, across Canada, Scandinavia, Siberia, and some of northernmost China and Japan. These forests account for 29 per cent of the world's forest cover, and approximately fourteen million square kilometres of the Earth's land area. Summers are short and cool, winters long and cold, and snow lies on the ground for half the year.

To the south, if the climate is sufficiently wet, lie the temperate forests from where we have just come, or extensive grasslands if we happen to be in the more arid continental regions. Had we taken the overland route from the temperate forests of Western Europe to the boreal regions of the north we would not have noticed any obvious transition, but rather a gradual change from one forest type to another. To the north, should we be so inclined to go that far, we would eventually reach the treeless tundra where permanently frozen soil combined with low summer temperatures prevent widespread tree establishment.

Across their vast range boreal forests can seem remarkably uniform in structure and composition. Almost everywhere the forest canopy comprises trees of just four conifer genera, spruce (*Picea*), pine (*Pinus*), fir (*Abies*), and larch (*Larix*). Broadleaved trees such as birch, poplar (*Populus*), and alder (*Alnus*) are present, but they are usually associated with recently burned areas. Many of these species almost, but not quite, span the globe at these latitudes. These immense ranges, coupled with the paucity of species, suggest a rather unchanging and monotonous forest type. The monotony is belied by a complex mix of shrubby plant communities that vary greatly according to topography, soil, and local climate. Boreal forests also encompass a great many lakes, forested wetlands, bogs, and meadows of various sizes scattered throughout the biome (Figure 13).

Surprisingly in such a cold environment, fire plays a major role in the boreal system. Periods of unseasonably dry and warm weather can generate fires that are often small in scale, but can occasionally cover 200,000 hectares or more. Fire frequency and extent varies greatly, even within a particular region, and so boreal forest landscapes often comprise a mosaic of patches in different stages of recovery and maturity.

Forests' end

Beyond the taiga is treeless tundra. Our tour thus concluded, let us not assume that forests can be so easily segregated by broad

13. **Boreal forest at Scotty Creek, Northwest Territories, Canada. Forests overlie permafrost areas, while the surrounding treeless wetlands are permafrost free.**

patterns in rainfall, seasonality, and temperature alone. I can enjoy a short walk from my home in central Europe that would take me through both beech forest and mixed conifer woodland, and within a short drive I could be walking through valleys clothed in sweet chestnut forest, or on mountain slopes surrounded by stands of spruce. On a slightly more serious hike during my annual Scottish Highland sojourn I could take in ancient pine forest, dry ash woodlands, and temperate oak rainforests—each woodland type determined more by soil and underlying geology than climate, although past management also makes an important contribution. Forests are highly diverse in form and composition, and typologies that simplify such complexity should not be taken too literally.

Chapter 3
Forest origins

Plants, of sorts, first started flourishing on dry land on ancient Precambrian coastlines around 600 million years ago (Mya). These early colonizers were lichens—associations of algae and fungi. True plants, in the form of mosses and liverworts, came much later at around 450 Mya, but these were, and still are, small organisms that are incapable of supporting a substantial structure. The origins of forests lie in the evolution of a key innovation some 400 Mya: water-conducting canals stiffened with a tough polymer called lignin. These strengthened water-conducting vessels provided structural support that allowed the early small and prostrate plants to increase their size and stand erect. The arborescent form, the single most important precondition for forest formation, was born.

The first forests

An arborescent form provided substantial benefits to plants, principally by providing better access to light for photosynthesis over prostrate non-lignified competitors. As soils began to accumulate and roots evolved into more complex forms that could penetrate deeper in search of groundwater, the plants that we can now begin to call trees began to spread away from the edges of water bodies. By around 385 Mya trees had spread widely across the globe to form the first forests. This had far-reaching implications. Probing plant roots coupled with substantially increased production of organic acids by the now extensive forests increased rates of rock weathering by orders of magnitude and accelerated soil formation (Box 3). Plant roots and organic acids further accelerated the weathering of silicates from rocks causing carbon dioxide to be locked up in ocean sediments. The concentration of atmospheric carbon dioxide (CO_2) plummeted tenfold over the next one hundred million years through the Carboniferous, additionally facilitated by the assimilation of atmospheric CO_2 into plant tissue within the expanding forests. This plant tissue could not be readily broken down, as lignin was highly resistant to decay. The accumulating organic matter was, instead, gradually buried, transformed, and locked up in the form of coal, resulting in near-permanent removal of vast quantities of carbon from the atmosphere. Our modern industrial civilizations, built on the exploitation of these coal reserves, owe their existence to the evolution of lignin and the first global forests, and our current climate change problems owe their origins to our reversal of a process that began some 380 Mya. But we are getting ahead of ourselves.

Box 3 Plants as rock breakers

The evolution and spread of land plants was a seminal event in the history of life. It heralded, of course, the emergence of a terrestrial biosphere, but it also had major implications for the atmosphere and geosphere. Plants increase the rate of rock weathering. The emergence of land plants, particularly during the Carboniferous, greatly accelerated rock weathering, a process by which calcium and magnesium silicates are, together with carbon dioxide, reconfigured to calcium and magnesium carbonates and silicon dioxide (quartz). Weathering draws down CO_2 from the atmosphere and locks it away, as calcium or magnesium carbonates, in the ocean depths. From the mid-Devonian through the Carboniferous (around 385–300 Mya) this process caused a tenfold drop in atmospheric CO_2, and permanent changes to the global climate.

Plants were the root cause of these changes. Plant roots secrete organic acids to break down minerals for nutrient acquisition. Carbonic acids from the decomposition of plant litter also contribute to the dissolution of minerals. Circulation of water by transpiration and its retention by organically rich soils increases water–mineral contact time, and hence extends favourable conditions for mineral breakdown.

These features are common to all terrestrial vascular plants, but it is the Carboniferous emergence of trees with massively enlarged root systems and greatly increased biomass production that accelerated weathering rates, and the drawing down of atmospheric CO_2, by orders of magnitude. Moreover, the burial of lignified wood, which resisted decomposition, and its subsequent conversion to coal, also made a considerable contribution to declining atmospheric CO_2 through this period.

The Earth's oldest forests date back to the Middle Devonian (385 Mya). We know this because in the 1920s hundreds of fossil tree stumps were discovered in an upright life position in a quarry near Gilboa, New York. The later association of these fossil stumps to fossilized leaf branches has allowed the reconstruction of the 'first tree', *Eospermatopteris*. Accompanying these large lignified but non-woody trees were scrambling woody vines and an arborescent member of the Lycopsida (clubmosses), a group that was to rise to greater prominence in the Carboniferous. Although fossil evidence for this earliest period of forest history is limited to only a few localities, it seems that several species of reasonably tall trees were well established and widespread in low latitude warm temperate zones by the Middle Devonian (Figure 14).

14. The first forests from the Devonian, comprising Eospermatopteris and other trees of the extinct Cladoxylopsida group.

These forests would have been quiet. There were as yet no land vertebrates and the first insects were only just beginning to evolve. There were, however, a variety of tiny detritus-eating springtails and millipedes, and predatory spider-like arthropods and centipedes. Worms and snails were probably present, but because they do not preserve well as fossils we know little about them. The earliest insects emerged in the Middle Devonian forests, as did true spiders and terrestrial scorpions. Devonian trees were, however, free of the scourge of herbivores, as no organism had yet evolved the capacity to digest the cellulose and lignin that forms plant tissues. Herbivores only achieved this feat much later by acquiring specialized gut microbes.

Forests were certainly widespread in the Carboniferous (359–299 Mya)—we have plenty of evidence for this in the form of coal deposits around the world. These early forests comprised a variety of 'trees' of between ten and thirty-five metres in height, with trunks up to one meter in diameter. Some of these would have been relatively familiar to us, including ten-metre tree ferns that would not have appeared out of place in the modern temperate rainforests of New Zealand, South Africa, or Australia. Most tree groups of the late Devonian and Carboniferous, however, bore little relation to modern forest taxa, which had yet to evolve in any recognizable form, or at all. Even so, some of these formerly arborescent groups still have extant and common, albeit diminutive, relatives.

A common tree of the Carboniferous was *Lepidodendron*, a giant clubmoss and distant relative of the still living *Lycopodium* genus. Fossil groves of early *Lepidodendron* forests have been uncovered in several locations, the most famous and easily accessible of which is in Victoria Park, Glasgow. Here, the application of a little imagination to the eleven fossil *Lepidodendron* stumps preserved in life position takes us back to the ancient Carboniferous forests. Other Carboniferous trees included giant relatives of modern horsetails. One of these, *Calamites*, achieved heights of around twenty metres, but was otherwise similar in form to the modern horsetails that are familiar to us as small herbaceous plants in forest undergrowth and gardens worldwide. By the late Carboniferous (315–299 Mya) these tree-sized clubmosses and horsetails formed dense and extensive lowland swamp forests that may have accounted for two-thirds of global forest cover. It is these forests that put the carbon in Carboniferous, and gave us the immense coal deposits that powered the industrial revolution.

Other Carboniferous tree groups have had a more lasting evolutionary legacy. Principal among these are the Progymnosperms, from which all modern seed plants evolved, and which are thus the early progenitors of our modern forests. Progymnosperms had a stem structure that resembled modern day conifers, and extensive deep root systems, lateral branches, and long leaves that were adapted to dry conditions. These traits allowed them to extend their range beyond lowland swamp forests to occupy higher and drier ground. They are well represented in the Carboniferous fossil record and number up to twenty genera. Some members of this group, such as *Archaeopteris*, actually date back to the mid-Devonian. As such *Archaeopteris* vies with *Eospermatopteris* for the 'first tree' title.

Unlike seed-bearing modern conifers and flowering plants, progymnosperms reproduced by spores. Yet by the late Carboniferous seed-bearing trees had evolved, though confusingly they are not ancestors of our modern seed plants. The Cordaites (330–250 Mya) were perhaps the tallest trees of Carboniferous and Permian forests, and fossil trunks have been measured at thirty metres. Another group of seed-bearing plants, the pteridosperms, resembled modern tree ferns (to which they are unrelated) and achieved heights of ten metres. So at the height of the Carboniferous and extending into the Permian extensive lowland swamp forests of horsetails, tree ferns, and clubmosses covered much of the Earth's land surface, while the drier higher ground supported a diverse array of progymnosperms and seed plants belonging to at least two evolutionary groups.

Transition and death of the early forests

The Permian was a period of transition. Towards the end of the Permian the early forests that had dominated the globe for the best part of one hundred million years underwent a change in composition as new plant types evolved and replaced earlier forms. This transition was gradual, spanning a thirty-million-year period (roughly 280–250 Mya) that straddles the Permian–Triassic boundary. Forests characterized by giant horsetails, ferns, Cordaites, and pteridosperms (Figure 15) gradually came to be dominated by new forms of seed-bearing plants that evolved from progymnosperm ancestors. This included several major groups that remain extant today such as the conifers and cycads. The Ginkgoales, the sole extant species of which is the maidenhair tree

15. This canopy of Rebecca's tree ferns (*Cyathea rebeccae*) from Eungella, Australia, might be similar to what the late Permian forests looked like.

Ginkgo biloba (beloved of urban planners on account of its toleration of pollution), also thrived during the Permian (Figure 16).

Over this period the total diversity of tree families declined by around 50 per cent (from thirty to fifteen families). The gradual nature of this change implies that the sudden end-Permian extinction (252 Mya) that caused the loss of around 70 per cent of terrestrial animal species had little obvious effect on plant evolution. Nonetheless, the end-Permian extinction event did cause widespread and catastrophic environmental changes. The extent of forests as a whole, regardless of their composition, declined greatly. Indeed, no coal deposits are known from the early Triassic, a period often referred to as the 'coal gap', suggesting the absence of former swamp forests. Sedimentary rocks of the early Triassic also indicate that sedimentation rates were far higher than at any time in the Permian. This implies much greater erosion, something that is unlikely had forests been extensive. Moreover, early Triassic climates were very arid. All this points to a widespread and rapid decline of forests following the Permian extinction event, although the evolutionary transition in forest species had been underway for many millions of years before this.

The early Triassic landscape was largely devoid of forests altogether, and even trees must have been scarce. This is the only time since the evolution of the first trees that forests were absent as one of Earth's biomes. After a delay of some five to ten million years forests recovered, and when they did it was the recently evolved conifers, cycads, and ginkgoes that dominated. The giant horsetails, Cordaites, and pteridosperms were gone.

Rise of seed plants

Modern seed plants primarily comprise the gymnosperms (conifers) and the angiosperms (flowering plants) which together account for all forests worldwide. They have their origins in the environmental changes during the Permian (299–252 Mya) wrought by the coalescing of the world's land masses into the single supercontinent Pangaea. The formation of Pangaea affected global climate in complex ways, but essentially it got warmer and drier, and atmospheric CO_2 concentrations rose. It is against this background that the seed plants evolved. Early seed plants included the Cycadales, represented today by around 100 species in tropical and warm temperate regions of the world, and the Bennettitales, an extinct group superficially similar to cycads but probably a distinct evolutionary line.

The gymnosperms, or conifers, including the Ginkgoales (Figure 16), although present in the Permian, increased greatly in species number and abundance during the Triassic (252–201 Mya) when the modern conifer families first evolved and diversified. The boreal conifer forests of Canada and northern Russia, the podocarp forests of New Zealand, *Araucaria* forests

16. Fossil leaf of an ancient ginkgo (*Ginkgo cordilobata*) from the Early Jurassic of Ishpushta, Afghanistan, about 190 million years before the present.

of Chile, and globally widespread cool temperate pine forests all trace their origins to the Triassic.

The flowering plants, or angiosperms, had their origins in the Cretaceous (around 125 Mya) but did not become dominant components of the world's forests until the early Tertiary (66 Mya). They are now our most familiar forest trees, comprising most species in temperate forests and almost all tropical forest species. It is not, however, entirely clear to what the angiosperms owe their success, or their late appearance.

Their evolution and spread was preceded by the break-up of Pangaea through the Jurassic (201–145 Mya) into northern Laurasia and southern Gondwana, and the subsequent further fragmentation of these continents. One idea proposes that, after a period of global cooling in the late Triassic, increased volcanism associated with Pangaea's break-up pumped greenhouse gases into the atmosphere creating much warmer environmental conditions that favoured angiosperms. Another theory, immediately attractive by virtue of its implication of dinosaurs, argues that a shift in dinosaur feeding behaviour from browsing the canopies of mature coniferous trees to snipping young conifer saplings restricted conifer regeneration, which provided opportunities for fast-growing angiosperms to establish. Unfortunately, the evidence seems stacked against this theory as fossil records suggest poor spatial overlap of the earliest angiosperms with the herbivore dinosaur groups purported to be responsible for their establishment.

A third and popular theory proposes that insects, not dinosaurs, were responsible for the great diversification of the flowering plants. Flowers evolved to attract insect pollinators. Insects seeking floral resources are far more efficient agents of genetic exchange than the wind currents on which the gymnosperms depend. The diversification of flowering plants might, therefore, be linked to insect diversification. Fossil evidence for insect–plant coevolution is ambiguous, as the timing of angiosperm diversification and that of major flower-visiting insect groups does not match closely. Some pollinator groups, particularly bees and moths, may have contributed to the evolution of certain angiosperm groups, but the timing of angiosperm evolution as a whole cannot be easily associated with that of insects.

Finally, a recent theory proposes that declining atmospheric CO_2 through the Cretaceous drove the evolution, among angiosperms, of much denser leaf venation which substantially improved the capacity of leaves to assimilate CO_2. Denser leaf venation would also have boosted the ability of plants to supply water to their chloroplasts. The net result is higher growth rates, allowing the angiosperms to successfully compete with, and slowly displace, conifers and other gymnosperms. Higher transpiration rates may also have humidified the atmosphere and increased rain in continental rainforest areas creating a self-reinforcing feedback.

The second age of forests

We cannot hope to understand the distribution and variety of present-day forests if we do not consider the past sixty-six million years. During this time the continents moved to their present locations, creating mountain ranges such as the Himalayas, the Alps, and the Andes. This drove major evolutionary radiations among many angiosperm groups. Global climate changed from being very warm to increasingly cool, culminating eventually in the series of great Ice Ages, a climatically favourable period of which we currently find ourselves. Sea levels rose and fell several times.

Against this backdrop angiosperms continued to diversify and populate forests with new species. Forests themselves extended from pole to pole from the late Palaeocene to early Eocene (around 60–50 Mya) and tropical or subtropical rainforest extended over most landmasses creating the largest extent of such forest that has ever existed, at least since the swamp forests of the Carboniferous some 300 million years earlier.

Forests that we would recognize today as having a wet tropical physiognomy extended well into the temperate latitudes, across present-day southern and western North America as well as most of Africa, South America, Australia, and South and South East Asia. The rest of the modern day United States, and most of Europe and Asia, was clothed with subtropical seasonally wet forests that comprised an unusual mix of temperate and tropical taxa. The coasts were fringed with mangroves as far north as Great Britain and as far south as Tasmania. Even Antarctica was covered with forests typical of temperate regions today. These mainly comprised evergreen coniferous trees such as araucarias and podocarps that still persist in Chile, Argentina, New Zealand, and Australia, and broadleaved southern beeches. Northern polar forests of mainly deciduous flowering trees, deciduous conifers, and some ginkgos extended to the northern coasts of Europe, Asia, and North America.

Major tectonic shifts in the distributions of continents in the Eocene (56–34 Mya) had important repercussions for global forests. The southern continents of Antarctica, South America, and Australasia began to break apart, and while Antarctica remained centred on the pole, South America and Australasia moved north towards their present positions.

By the early Oligocene (around 30 Mya) continental separation allowed the formation of a circumpolar ocean circulation system in the Southern Ocean that isolated Antarctica from warm equatorial currents. Antarctic temperatures plummeted, and the temperate forests that covered Antarctica declined and disappeared altogether under growing ice sheets. The opening up of the North Atlantic allowed cold Arctic waters to flow southwards, both cooling and drying the mid to high latitudes of the northern hemisphere and causing a retreat of forests from these areas. Mountain-building episodes between 55 and 40 Mya, including the uplift of the Himalayas, the Tibetan Plateau, and the Andes and Rocky Mountains, further contributed to global cooling and aridity, a trend that has continued from the Eocene some 50 Mya to the present day (or at least until human activities began to warm global climates).

As a result of these tectonic and climatic changes forest formations began to shrink back from high latitudes. Cold-tolerant pines had replaced broadleaved forests in polar latitudes by around 35 Mya, while the beginnings of Antarctic glaciation led to a rapid contraction and eventual disappearance of trees from the continent. Wet evergreen tropical forests began to retreat from central Eurasia and North America to be replaced with drier mixed evergreen and deciduous forest formations. Tropical rainforests contracted to more or less their current distribution by around 10 Mya.

At around this time the first grasses appeared. While seemingly insignificant, this event had profound implications for forests worldwide. Grasses resist drought by preferentially investing in root growth, and by a number of water-conserving morphological and physiological traits. Grasses also hold their growing tips at the base of leaf blades close to the soil which allows them to recover rapidly from fire and grazing. The shift towards a drier and cooler climate from the late Eocene (from around 47 Mya) favoured grasses. An increased propensity of fires and the evolution of immense herds of mammalian herbivores, both perhaps facilitated by the spread of grasslands, further favoured grasses which could rapidly recover from such impacts. Grassland savannahs, often still with woody tree components, spread in tropical and subtropical regions. Extensive temperate grasslands began to exclude forests from seasonally dry continental interiors at mid-latitudes giving rise to the prairies of North America, the steppes of Eurasia, the South American pampas, and the grassveld of southern Africa.

Quaternary Ice Ages

The reduction in atmospheric CO_2 concentration since the Eocene eventually allowed the formation of large ice sheets in the northern hemisphere, and the first of a series of Ice Age episodes began around 2.5 Mya. At least ten cycles of glaciation have occurred, with long glaciated periods punctuated by comparatively short and warm interglacial periods. Ice Age conditions were not only far colder, but also more arid. These conditions decimated forests in Europe and North America. Europe was covered with treeless tundra and forests were only able to hang on in isolated pockets (or refugia) in Iberia and south-eastern Europe. Much of northern Asia was too dry to allow the accumulation of ice and so remained ice free, but it was also too dry for extensive forests. The eastern United States was, however, able to support pine and spruce woodlands, and forests also persisted in Japan.

The cooler temperatures of the Pleistocene Ice Ages reduced oceanic evaporation, and hence atmospheric humidity. The resulting arid conditions caused the drying out of subtropical woodlands and tropical forests. In Africa savannahs expanded and tropical rainforest formations were reduced to a fraction of their former size. Deserts extended their range. West Africa and Florida, where tropical and subtropical forests exist today, were covered with extensive savannahs. Similar, but less pronounced changes occurred in South America and South East Asia.

In South East Asia higher elevation areas would have supported drier and more open forests where once there was (and now is again) rainforest. Nonetheless, sea levels were around one hundred metres lower than the present day, and hence much of South East Asia's continental shelf was then exposed as land on which rainforests persisted. The decline of tropical rainforests in upland areas during glacial episodes is likely to have been compensated by their expansion in lowland areas exposed by sea level lowering. The return of the wetter and warmer interglacial in which we now find ourselves ushered a reversal of this pattern.

The warmer and wetter interglacial periods also saw the return and expansion of forests across Europe. Relatively open boreal forests of birch, pine, and other conifers were able to establish in central and northern Europe. Oaks may have started to expand out of their localized southern refugia, only to be confined again to patchy southern regions when dry glacial conditions returned.

Our modern forests

We can trace the formation of our modern forests from the end of the last glacial period, some ten to twelve thousand years before present (BP), through the Holocene. Indeed, the return of forests across northern Europe and North America in the wake of a warming climate and glacial retreat is a great story of natural history told through the study of fossil pollen (Box 4). In this

Box 4 Palynology: pollen speaks

How do we know the sequence in which trees spread back into northern latitudes at the end of the last Ice Age? We can make reasonable estimates by analysing the relative abundance of pollen grains trapped within peat deposits or lake sediments.

Pollen is highly resistant to degradation, and is also produced in huge quantities. Each year, in temperate forests, up to ten metric tonnes of pollen can be produced from one square kilometre of forest. Pollen from different species is also distinctive, and so analysis of pollen (palynology) within sediments provides a reasonable time sequence of the relative abundance of tree species in the local area.

Of course, some trees, such as wind-pollinated pines, produce far more pollen than, say, insect-pollinated holly. Nevertheless, we can usually correct for these differences. Knowing whether the tree species represented by fossil pollen formed mixed forest or separate stands is more difficult. Radiocarbon dating provides a means of fixing fossil pollen layers in time, and a sequence of analyses of different sedimentary layers allows the reconstruction of past vegetation.

Pollen-based vegetation histories can also be used to derive estimates of past climates. Different plant species are restricted to certain ranges of temperature and rainfall and so can act as proxies of past climates. Using the relative distributions of fossil pollen, climatic maps for different times in the past have been produced for North America. Climatic reconstruction of Europe has proved more difficult on account of the long history of human impact which has profoundly affected species composition. Nonetheless, the human land use signature can also be tracked through macrofossils in the form of charred seeds or wood charcoal, and a sudden increase in these might correspond to increased forest use.

post-glacial Holocene period we must, however, contend not only with the effects of the changing climate on vegetation, but also with the influence of humans, which was felt almost the moment the retreating ice exposed the bare land to tree seeds and human footprints. The formation of the modern forests cannot be separated from the influence of agriculture, domestication, wood use (both timber and fuel wood), and the use of fire.

The return of forests to northern climes was remarkably rapid following the retreating ice after 12,000 BP. Pollen records (Figure 17) tell us that around 11,500 BP, at the start of the Holocene, deciduous trees began to expand out of their southern refugia. Many short-lived woodland communities that have no modern analogue became established. Their composition reflected the haphazard colonization of an empty land by tree species limited only by their dispersal capacities, and largely unconstrained by ecological processes of competition that would shape later forest communities. Juniper (*Juniperus*), willow (*Salix*), birch, aspen, and pine were the early colonizers from around 10,500 BP. They were quickly followed and to a large extent displaced northwards by hazel (*Corylus*), oak, and elm which, by 9,000 BP, had become widely established across Europe.

By 8,000 BP, deciduous forests spanned northern Europe to the British Isles and southern Scandinavia, pushing the birch-pine boreal forest to northern Scandinavia and Russia. New arrivals such as ash, lime, and alder began to infiltrate European forests from around 7,000 BP, while oak continued to spread. Late arrivals included beech and spruce, both probably continuing to extend their ranges even today. Oak and pinewood forests also spread across the Mediterranean, as did olive and pistachio (*Pistacia*). By around 4,000 BP the distribution and composition of the main forest types of Europe was similar to what we are currently familiar with.

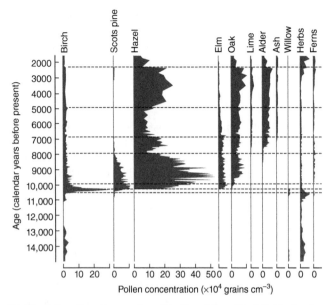

Forest origins

17. **Absolute pollen diagram from Hockham Mere, Norfolk, England.**
By comparing the relative abundances of pollen in sediments it is possible
to determine the ebb and flow of different tree species through the
Holocene. In this example, soon after the retreat of the glaciers there was
an explosion of birch, closely followed by pine and hazel. Elm and oak
arrived sometime later and began to displace birch and pine, while hazel
presumably persisted in the understorey. This mix was supplemented at
intervals with other incoming species, though since 6,000 years ago
forest composition in Norfolk has remained fairly stable.

Much the same process unfolded in North America, though it
started somewhat earlier and, in some areas, finished later than in
Europe. The actors were also different. Warming at the end of the
Pleistocene (after around 18,000 BP) thinned the depth of the ice
sheet, but did not cause significant retreat of ice cover which
extended south to a latitude of 40 degrees. Boreal forest was
distributed across most of eastern North America, with temperate
deciduous forests being confined to warmer southern climes
around the Gulf of Mexico.

The ice sheet finally began to slowly retreat after 14,000 BP. Mixed conifer-deciduous forests and more southerly temperate deciduous forests, comprising species such as oak, hemlock (*Tsuga*), hickory (*Carya*), and sweet chestnut (*Castanea*), started to expand their range. Boreal forest was pushed north, and in some cases right up to the edges of the ice sheets.

The eventual melting of the ice by 6,000 BP finally allowed the compressed boreal zone to extend northwards to occupy its current distribution. A simultaneously drying climate facilitated the eastward expansion of grasslands and herbs which confined temperate deciduous forests to eastern North America reflecting, more or less, their modern distributions.

We know less about vegetation transformations in the tropics following the Ice Ages. The tropics certainly became wetter and warmer, and many desert regions of West and East Africa gradually became more wooded. The Sahara Desert did not exist in anywhere near its present extent during the early Holocene (9,000–5,000 BP), and was instead covered by dry savannah woodlands where, as ancient rock paintings and carvings illustrate, giraffe, lions, antelope, elephants, hippos, and crocodiles roamed (Figure 18).

Retreating ice sheets resulted in rising sea levels which swamped many low-lying tropical areas causing the extent of tropical rainforest in South East Asia to decline dramatically simply because of a loss of land area to marine incursions. Forests did, however, pursue the retreating glaciers up mountains in East Africa, New Guinea, and the Andes. Dry forest and savannah corridors in central Africa, South East Asia, and the Amazon were claimed once more by tropical rainforests. Areas of the South American lowlands that had been dominated by non-wooded vegetation during the Pleistocene gradually became more wooded.

Pollen cores from Carajas, Lake Pata, and marine deposits off the mouth of the Amazon River, suggest that central Amazonian

18. Ancient rock art depicting giraffes from Tassili-n-Ajer, southern Algeria. This painting is thought to date to around 5,000 years ago and implies much wetter conditions capable of supporting these savannah woodland species.

rainforests remained largely intact during the Pleistocene and it is unlikely that they ever contracted to only a few isolated refugia from which they subsequently expanded, as has been popularly suggested. Since 5,000 BP African forests might have become less extensive following reduced solar insolation and associated temperature reductions linked to the Earth's axial precession, but major changes in the distribution of tropical moist forests have probably not been very substantial.

The (un)natural forests

The glacial ice of the Swiss Alps has stories to tell. In the hot summer of 2003, some 2,750 metres high on the Schnidejoch Pass, curious objects were disgorged from the melting ice. Being 300 metres above the tree line these wooden objects had no right to be there, unless left there by someone. The objects turned out to be arrow shafts and a birch-bark quiver of Neolithic age, and that someone must therefore be around 5,000 years old. The ice of Canada's remote northern Yukon Territory is even more obliging, and has revealed a treasure trove of ancient artefacts that include a 9,000-year-old wooden spear. A Neolithic longbow complete with arrows, dated to 6,000 BP, has been recovered from melting ice in Norway's Oppdal Mountains, and wooden fragments far above the tree line in Russia's far-east are indicative of ancient reindeer-hunting expeditions.

The conclusion is inescapable: people have been exploiting the wood and animal resources of the alpine and boreal forests since these forests first expanded into lands exposed by the retreating Ice Age. Remote as the boreal forests are, hugging the fringes of the Arctic Circle and almost at the inhospitable northern limits of land's extent, humans have been using and moving through them for millennia, and in so doing they have been shaping the density, distribution, and composition of trees in these areas.

The same is true of temperate areas. In these regions the use of fire, livestock domestication and herding, and the cultivation of a variety of plants became widespread. These activities opened up forest stands and created opportunities for some tree species to spread. In Europe early human activity favoured fir, birch, and spruce and, in the Mediterranean, pine. As Neolithic people removed competing species, favoured trees such as walnut (*Juglans*), pistachio, and olive became far more widespread than would otherwise have been the case. Woodland clearance by Neolithic humans has been blamed for the spread of elm disease that caused the sudden decline of elm in Europe between 7,000 and 6,500 BP and its replacement with beech and hornbeam.

Thus in Europe, just as forests were extending northwards and thickening, Neolithic people and their domesticated animals were creating openings and clearances and, intentionally or otherwise, favouring some tree species over others. Humans have continued to modify forested landscapes, and the forests that we are familiar with today are as much a product of human intervention as of climatic change.

The not-so 'pristine' tropical forests

> We went among some islands which we thought uninhabited,
> but after we got to be in among them, so numerous were the
> settlements which came into sight...that we grieved.

So wrote the missionary Gaspar de Carvajal on 25 June 1542 in his chronicle of the first Spanish expedition down the Amazon River. In addition to numerous villages, the settlements that he was so disappointed to see included fortified towns with broad, well-maintained roads and large populations. The Amazon basin, at least along the extensive river margins, was certainly not empty of people—indeed quite the opposite. Population estimates of indigenous peoples in the New World prior to European conquests of the early 16th century have recently been revised substantially upwards to between forty-three and sixty-five million. Such populations had to be supported by extensive agriculture, as is indeed indicated by eyewitness accounts of early European settlers, and as evidenced by layers of burned organic materials and pottery shards within many American soils.

The reality of tropical forests that are seasonally dry or close to rivers is that they have been worked over, cleared, burned, and cut for as long as humans have been around. Archaeological evidence demonstrates large-scale landscape transformation in many parts of the seasonal Amazon centuries before European arrival. In the southern Amazon, for example, substantial archaeological evidence points to human occupation of the Upper Xingu region (within a 400-square-kilometre area) over a period spanning 1,000 years, with initial colonization starting around 1,500 BP. Settlements were set within intensively managed agricultural areas and connected by formally arranged road networks. These archaeologically mapped areas correspond to distinct forest types that include many fruit trees associated with unusually fertile '*terra preta*' soils (Box 5).

The concept of vast tracts of pristine tropical forest never exposed to human exploitation is now recognized to be mostly a myth. Almost wherever we look tropical forests show signs of having been affected to greater or lesser extents by a long history of human interventions, often limited only to hunting and occasional occupation, but sometimes extending to large-scale forest clearance to support urbanized civilizations.

We should, however, take care not to extend this interpretation too far. Extensive human land use change has been largely confined to seasonally dry regions of the tropics, or along river channels. Large swathes of aseasonal tropical forests have been substantially, if not entirely, shaped by natural forces, with indiscernible human impact. Moreover, long periods of natural regeneration following light and brief human occupation have resulted in forest formations in which humankind's legacy is cryptic at best. Even relatively substantial human transformation

Box 5 *Terra preta*: the rich forest soils of the Amazon

Across the Amazon curious patches of highly fertile dark soils bear little resemblance to surrounding weathered infertile soils. These *terra preta de Indio* (Indian black earth) are a legacy of pre-Columbian cultivation dating as far back as 4,500 years.

Terra preta can cover a few to more than 300 hectares and often exceeds two metres in depth. They have been made fertile by the addition of large quantities of crumbled charcoal, ash, green manure, and, in some cases, fish meal. Ceramic and bone fragments attests to their human origins.

Terra preta sites are also associated with fruit trees and other useful species, further reflecting a human legacy. There is debate as to whether the soil improvement was intended or inadvertent—resulting from land clearing practices and waste disposal—or a combination of both. In either case, the fertility of *terra preta* supported high pre-Columbian population densities in the heart of what is now the Amazon forest, and their existence punctures 'virgin rainforest' myths.

of forests can be quickly erased as forests reclaim abandoned land. In 1525 the Spanish conquistador Hernán Cortés spent many weeks hacking his way through tropical forests in Mayan territory in modern-day southern Mexico and Guatemala, and while he encountered many small family settlements dispersed in the forest, as well as the island city of Nojpetén, he also stumbled across the ruins of long-abandoned ancient Mayan cities that had been completely overwhelmed by centuries-old forests (Figure 19).

Forests established on land that was once cleared of forest are termed 'secondary' to distinguish them from 'primary' forests that have never been completely cleared. Of course, if we go back far enough most forests have regrown at some point. Many central

19. The Mayan ruins of Tikal, Guatemala, claimed by rainforest after
its abandonment some 1,000 years ago.

African forests appear to be only 2,500 years old, and Mexico's southern Yucatan forests date from the collapse of the Maya around 1,000 years ago. European settlement of Puerto Rico in the early 1500s was accompanied by near complete forest clearance, though widespread abandonment of agricultural land from the 1940s initiated forest regrowth to the current 45 per cent forest cover, more than three-quarters of which is not even fifty years old. In time, the structure and composition of secondary forests grade into formations that are almost indistinguishable from 'primary' formations, and just where to draw the line between primary and secondary forests is difficult to determine objectively.

We should not necessarily abandon 'natural' forest as a concept. A broader definition of 'natural' that is appropriate in the context of our human-dominated landscapes is that of forest derived through a process of unassisted reproduction, establishment, and growth and which consists of naturally immigrant tree species. The FAO uses a different definition of natural forest where 'naturalness' describes the degree of resemblance to a condition that might have existed in the absence of human intervention. As FAO itself recognizes, the problem with such a definition is that we have no obvious reference point, partly because there is no such undisturbed forest.

Naturalness, therefore, more usefully refers to woodlands that express natural forest dynamics, including tree composition, occurrence of dead wood, mixed age structure, and natural regeneration processes, over an area that is large enough to maintain these natural characteristics, and where the last significant human intervention was sufficiently long ago to have allowed natural species compositions and processes to become established. As we shall see, however, forests are highly dynamic and changeable independent of any human intervention, and identifying any single 'natural' state can be fraught with difficulty.

Chapter 4
Disturbance and dynamics

Forests are in a constant state of change, and the natural state of any given woodland applies only, to borrow a phrase from Thomas Hardy, 'at this point of time, at this point of space'. Some perturbations are dramatic, such as forest fires or storms. Others, such as tree diseases, spread slowly through a forest and are both chronic and cryptic. Forest management has often sought to protect forests from such disturbances, but in the process we have disrupted processes of change that are very much integral to the functioning of forest ecosystems. To appreciate how dynamic forests really are, we need to follow the life of a forest over the course of a few decades.

Forty years of change in Lady Park Wood

Lady Park Wood in Wales has probably never been completely cleared. This is not to say that it is entirely natural, as the woodland has been managed for centuries by favouring tall oak and beech while coppicing ash, elm, and lime to form the understorey wood. Since 1902, however, the woodland has been left almost entirely unmanaged under a non-intervention policy. The absence of management over the course of a century provides an ideal opportunity to understand forest trajectories under near-natural conditions. It turns out that the fate of Lady Park

Wood, and many other temperate forests like it, is far from predictable. In the decades leading up to the 1970s, the rapidly growing beech trees came to dominate the woodland at the expense of other species. Shrubs gradually disappeared as the beech canopy closed over and greatly reduced light in the understorey. Beech was not able to establish everywhere though, as some parts of the woodland are located on steep slopes with thin soils that could not support beech. In such places regular tree falls allowed sufficient light to the understorey to support a vigorous shrub layer. Nonetheless, at this point it seemed that a large part of Lady Park Wood was developing into a mature beech forest.

A series of events changed all this. In the early 1970s disease started killing elm trees, which opened up the woodland canopy, benefitting fast-growing birch. A severe summer drought in 1976 killed many mature beech trees and created gaps in the canopy. These openings exposed many of the remaining beech trees to toppling by wind (windthrow), opening the canopy yet further. Birch was unable to take advantage as it too was severely weakened by the 1976 drought. A severe late snowfall in April 1981 crushed many surviving birch trees. The snow also pressed many young lime trees to the ground but these mostly recovered by producing new shoots from the fallen stems. In 1983 young beech shoots were gnawed and killed by grey squirrels, and two years later an exceptionally large vole outbreak killed almost all beech saplings. At the end of this series of events beech had been reduced to such an extent that the wood currently appears destined to be a predominantly ash and lime forest. Or at least it would be so were it not for the recent spread of ash dieback disease that is likely to greatly diminish the number and vigour of ash.

Forests are dynamic even over short human timescales. The recent history of Lady Park Wood, spanning no more than a few decades, illustrates how the species mix of woodlands naturally fluctuates, in this case between beech dominance and ash–lime dominance, according to the chance occurrence of various climatic and biological disturbances. Some of these disturbances, such as the late snowfall event that lasted no more than a couple of days, are exceedingly brief, while others, such as elm or ash diseases, are more chronic and even permanent. Both, however, leave lasting legacies that affect woodland dynamics and make it extremely difficult to predict with any certainty the longer-term structure and composition of woodlands.

As Lady Park Wood shows, many different kinds of disturbances afflict forests, and they exert strong control over forest composition and structure. The disturbance regime, that is the type, frequency, and severity of all disturbances a forest is exposed to, will determine whether the forest is dominated by young trees of fast-growing species, or old trees that, in the absence of frequent severe disturbances, are able to slowly outcompete and eventually exclude other species. Disturbances do not affect all trees equally. Some species are, for example, well adapted to fire while others are entirely consumed. Disease is often highly species specific, allowing unaffected species to expand into areas formerly occupied by susceptible species. Strong winds tend to knock over middle-aged trees leaving the largest and smallest trees mostly unaffected. Disturbance outcomes can also be a matter of luck, or lack of it—simply being in the wrong place at the wrong time.

Windstorms

Northern temperate forests, which occupy some of the windier regions of the globe, are regularly exposed to a variety of wind-related disturbance phenomena (Figure 20). Severe thunderstorms create downbursts of cold dense air that hit the ground and splay out in all directions. These discrete events cause significant tree damage under each downburst, creating patches of damaged forest along the path of the thunderstorm. On occasion, extensive damage can be caused by particularly powerful

20. Windthrown Norway spruce (*Picea abies*) in the Bavarian National Park, Germany.

storms. The 1977 Flambeau Blowdown in northern Wisconsin, comprising twenty-six separate downburst events, removed over 50 per cent of the canopy in 140,000 hectares of forest. This storm, and two similar storms in 1995 and 1999, both in northern Minnesota, are an order of magnitude larger than those observed in historical data, implicating climate change in exacerbating the size and severity of these storms.

Cyclones devastate tropical forests near coasts, such as Australia's Wet Tropics region. Severe forest damage is largely contained within fifty kilometres of the cyclone's track, and even within this zone damage is patchy at the landscape scale, with many areas of forest remaining intact. These intact forest areas are important seed sources for regeneration and provide refuge for forest animals, which facilitates the recovery of adjacent areas of damaged forest.

By some accounts, global warming is expected to increase the intensities of tropical cyclones by up to 20 per cent by the end of this century. If the consequence is more extensive forest damage, then forest recovery might be slower. Increasing cyclone severity might also favour species that are more resistant to strong winds, such as palms, and species that are more tolerant of disturbed conditions, such as fast-growing but short-lived trees as well as vines and weeds. Such shifts in composition change the nature of forests completely, affecting forest biodiversity as well as the cycling of nutrients, carbon, and water.

Fire

Along with water, earth, and air, the ancient Greeks considered fire as one of the classical elemental forces that shape the world around us. Generally, where there is vegetation there is fire. Forests are no exception, and vast areas of boreal and tropical dry forest owe their structure and composition to natural lightning-caused fire regimes. Humans have used fire for many millennia to manage wooded landscapes for their own needs. Australian landscapes, for example, have been shaped over tens of thousands of years by aboriginal peoples' use of fire. As a management tool fire can be corralled and directed, and its frequency controlled. Natural fires are altogether more haphazard. They vary in type and severity, in their spatial extent, and in frequency at any one location.

The large majority of natural fires burn through the litter on a forest floor consuming fallen leaves, twigs, stems, shed bark, and understorey vegetation such as grasses. These fires might be very light and slow moving, such that the fire front can be stepped over. If there is plenty of dry fuel and favourable winds, these light surface fires can rapidly build into intense fires that burn dead branch wood several metres above the forest floor. Much rarer are severe crown fires (Figure 21). These occur when a large surface fire leaps into the canopy creating a massive conflagration that rips through the tree tops. Such fires can extend over huge areas. In boreal forests a high-intensity crown

21. Fighting a forest fire with helicopter suppression in South Korea.

fire can easily burn 10,000 hectares, and occasionally more than 400,000 hectares. Surface fires are much more limited in extent, perhaps affecting no more than a few hectares and petering out whenever they encounter wetter areas, streams, roads, or artificially created fire breaks, where there is insufficient dry fuel to maintain the fire.

Forests are not uniformly flammable. In temperate hardwood forests dry litter and coarse woody debris will support light surface fires, but crown fires are very rare due to the relatively (compared to conifers) high leaf moisture content. Large intense canopy fires have occurred in northern temperate hardwood forests in the past (the Peshtigo Fire, Wisconsin, consumed around 500,000 hectares in October 1871), but only after accumulated fuel from logging slash had been dried by a period of dry weather. Modern forest management no longer allows extensive areas of logging slash to be left across the landscape, and so large fires in these forests are unlikely to occur again.

Northern conifer forests, by contrast, have dense canopy foliage and heavy understorey fuel loads. After dry spells these forests can experience intense crown fires with flame lengths exceeding twenty metres. Controlling such crown fires is not possible, and they only stop when they exhaust all the fuel, or when extinguished by rain or snowfall. It is said that people can start and stop surface fires, but they can only start crown fires. As a general rule, in the northern coniferous forests 97 per cent of the landscape is burned by the largest 3 per cent of fires. Fire suppression can thus extinguish 97 per cent of fires which would only anyway have affected 3 per cent of the landscape. Controlling the largest 3 per cent of fires is almost impossible, yet it is these fires that cause almost all the damage. Fire prevention has therefore been an important element of forest protection. In the United States, Smokey Bear, created in 1944 as a wildfire prevention icon, has engrained in generations of Americans the need to prevent, as opposed to control, wildfires.

Another relevant feature of the forest fire regime is the return interval, or the average frequency with which a fire returns to any particular location. In boreal forests fire rotations are on the order of fifty to one hundred years in western Canada and Alaska, rising to over 200 years in the wetter regions of eastern Canada. In the white spruce (*Picea glauca*) floodplain forests of the Canadian west fire rotations exceed 300 years, while in Europe fire return intervals of boreal forests in Sweden might be as infrequent as 500 years. Moist temperate forests generally burn far less frequently, although these forests have been so modified by human development that a natural fire regime no longer exists.

Fire rotations can also be very short. Jack pine (*Pinus banksiana*) barrens of the eastern United States and Canada burn every fifteen to twenty years. In the dry temperate forest zone California's mixed conifer forests and the longleaf pine (*Pinus palustris*) forests of south-eastern United States burn every two to twenty years. The fire interval of eastern Spain's Aleppo pine

(*Pinus halepensis*) forests is a little longer at around fifty years, while in California's giant sequoia (*Sequoiadendron giganteum*) forests the fire interval is much more variable at anything between ten and one hundred years. Tropical rainforests, by contrast, almost never burn, at least not naturally.

Some forests actually create conditions that favour fire. In Australia, volatile leaf oils, copious litter production, and highly flammable bark of eucalypt trees encourage and exacerbate fires that destroy competitors. In Australia's temperate rainforests, southern beech seedlings rapidly colonize the understory of *Eucalyptus regnans* forests to form a dense canopy beneath which the eucalypts cannot regenerate. Only after a fire opens the canopy, and triggers massive seed fall, are the eucalypts able to regenerate. Eucalypts are native to Australia but have been widely introduced to many other regions of the world including California, where they are blamed by many to be exacerbating dangerous wildfires.

Fire is an important agent of disturbance in dry tropical regions, and one to which trees are usually well adapted. Wet tropical forests which do not naturally burn can do so following logging activities and forest fragmentation. Even so, fire in disturbed rainforests is almost always set, deliberately or otherwise, by people. Once burned, even if only lightly, rainforests become far more flammable as the trees are not adapted to withstand fire. As they die they add to the fuel load creating conditions for far more serious fires. It is this positive feedback cycle that has caused the degradation of large areas of tropical rainforest in recent decades.

Herbivores and pests

In Disney's film *Bambi*, the eponymous young deer flees a great forest conflagration in terror, from which he is saved by his father, a magnificent deer stag. The great evil in the film is the fire that burns the forest, but a more insidious problem for many forests is not fire, but rather deer. Many species of deer, particularly white-tailed deer and moose in North America and red deer in Europe, browse young seedlings and saplings and in so doing greatly curtail the regeneration of trees. In Scotland high numbers of red deer pose a particular problem for the regeneration of Scots pine forests, some of which have not seen substantial pine regeneration for 300 years. Many smaller mammals, including mice, squirrels, voles, and rabbits, also regularly eat tree seeds and seedlings, sufficient to alter the course of woodland development, as we have seen at Lady Park Wood.

These animals have a preference for particular tree species, and can therefore potentially change woodland composition and future development. Moreover, some tree species can tolerate repeated browsing, but others not. Many broadleaved tree saplings, for example, will readily resprout if the leading stem is browsed, but conifers generally lack this ability. This is significant in the boreal zone where voles more than make up for the loss of the boreal megafauna (towards the end of the Pleistocene) by bulk in numbers. In northern Europe vole outbreaks occur on a three to four year cycle (and somewhat more irregularly in North America) during which populations multiply several hundredfold. As voracious feeders they rapidly consume their preferred plant roots and bulbs, and switch to seedlings of pines, spruces, and other conifers. This can have substantial economic impact for commercial forestry, and in Finland alone the cost of seedling losses to voles has been estimated at €20 million during such outbreaks.

Browsing mammals feed on trees, leaves, and shoots, and consequently suppress tree growth. Conversely, grazers feed on grasses and can enhance tree establishment. This is most obviously played out in the African plains. By supressing trees in African dry forests, elephants, giraffes, and other large browsers facilitate the spread and growth of grasses. This creates a substantial fuel load, and the resulting intense fires reduce woody vegetation further and prevent tree regeneration. Grazers such as zebra and wildebeest reverse this process by cropping the grasses which reduces fire intensity. Trees re-establish, and the resulting forest shade supresses the grasses. The oscillation of African savannahs from woodland to grassland is therefore maintained by different kinds of herbivores.

Yet it is predators that have the key role in triggering the change from woodlands to grasslands. Trees provide predators with cover within which they can stalk and ambush herbivores. Herbivores therefore exist within a 'landscape of fear' in which they avoid wooded areas in favour of more open grasslands where they can more easily spot predators. The concentration of grazing herbivores in grasslands is therefore mediated by predators, and this serves as the main driver of conversion to woodland. Elephants, by contrast, are more or less immune to predators on account of their bulk, and have no aversion to wooded areas. As large browsers they feed on leaves, breaking branches and even knocking over trees to get to them, thereby initiating a return to grassland.

No matter the destruction wrought by mammalian herbivores, it pales into insignificance compared to that caused by insects. Since 1990 some thirty billion conifers from Alaska to Mexico have been killed by diminutive bark beetles. Individually, bark beetles are smaller than a grain of rice, but when conditions are right their populations explode in epidemics that can last a decade or more. In recent decades a few bark beetle species, such as the mountain pine beetle (*Dendroctonus ponderosae*) in North America and the European spruce bark beetle (*Ips typographus*), have been particularly destructive of coniferous forests (Figure 22).

The increased incidence of summer droughts in these regions has rendered many trees vulnerable to attack, while milder winters have facilitated the growth of bark beetle populations. Healthy

22. The European bark beetle (*Ips typographus*), an adult (top)
and a gallery (bottom), from Switzerland.

trees defend themselves by drowning the tiny pine beetles in resin.
Female beetles therefore target vulnerable drought-stressed trees,
and once located they release a pheromone to attract other
beetles. The tree responds with resin and poisonous gases, but

sheer force of numbers eventually overcomes a tree's defences. The beetles, which might now number several thousand, lay their eggs under the bark and the larvae feed on the living tissue which ultimately kills the trees.

Whole forests have been devastated in North America, Norway, and Germany, transforming landscapes in the process, changing watershed hydrology, and leaving logging communities bereft. The first indications that the North American bark beetle epidemic might be in remission emerged in 2012, after more than two decades of pine beetle outbreak. Having devastated pine forests, the insect is running out of food.

Bark beetles are not alone among insect pests. Outbreaks of spruce budworm (various species of *Choristoneura*), a moth caterpillar, can last up to twenty-five years and can cause near complete mortality of pure balsam fir stands along the southern edge of North American boreal forests. Balsam fir is better protected when it occurs with other tree species as the budworm mainly kills the larger trees leaving younger and smaller trees largely unaffected, a pattern that ensures the persistence of fir in the forest.

In general, higher diversity of tree species confers increased protection from pests, which have more trouble finding suitable hosts among many species. Tropical forest trees that grow in highly species-rich forest are thus very rarely, if ever, afflicted by extensive pest outbreaks. Even if they were, any disease outbreak that happened to decimate a particular tree species would have marginal significance for the forest as a whole, as each tree species constitutes a small proportion of all tropical rainforest trees.

Disease

Insects are not alone among tree pests. In Europe the spruce bark beetle carries with it several species of fungus and mites, and various bacteria. Some of these can facilitate or exacerbate the destructive impact of the beetles, while others can be more destructive than the beetle itself. The mountain pine beetle infects trees with blue stain fungus on which its larvae prefer to feed as it is far more digestible than wood. Without the fungus, the impact of the mountain pine beetle would be greatly diminished. Dutch Elm disease, responsible for the near complete loss of mature elm trees across Europe since the late 1960s, is caused by a fungal pathogen spread by a mite that itself hitches a lift on the back of the elm bark beetle. In Britain, elm now survives only as severely reduced hedgerow bushes, while France has lost 90 per cent of its elm trees.

Ultimately, however, the source of many tree disease outbreaks can be traced to human trade. Dutch elm disease, for example, was brought into Europe by the shipment of infected logs from North America. In the first half of the 20th century chestnut blight, another fungus, devastated sweet chestnut forests in the eastern US (killing an estimated 3.5 billion trees) after being accidentally introduced from Asia. The latest disease to afflict British woodlands is *Chalara (Hymenoscyphus fraxineus)*, a deadly fungal pathogen of ash, introduced on seedlings imported by the tree nursery trade.

Tree pathogens rarely destroy forests but, by selectively decimating particular species, they change forest composition. They can be a boon for other tree species that fill in the gaps created by dead trees, and for understorey herbaceous species that quickly take advantage of openings in forest canopies. Birch, followed by maple, for example, were the beneficiaries of sweet chestnut declines in the eastern United States. On the other hand, species associated with afflicted trees may decline. The fate of the rich biodiversity of insects and lichens that are closely associated with ash in Britain is tied to that of the tree which, in the current context, pivots around the impact of *Chalara*. A small percentage of ash trees appear resistant to the disease, and it is possible, even likely, that over a few decades ash will slowly recover, as will its associated biodiversity, as seedlings from these resistant individuals establish and spread. Thus forest species composition is in a constant state of flux as trees are afflicted by diseases (and possibly eventually recover from them), and are supplanted by other species.

It is in tropical rainforests where pathogens have their most important, but also most subtle, effects in shaping forest composition. At high latitudes cold winters kill many pathogens, but in the tropics mild or non-existent winters allow pathogens to persist year round. Tree pathogens are most successful where high densities of their host plants allow the pathogen to spread rapidly from one individual to the next. As the large majority of seeds from any tree do not disperse far, seedling densities tend to be very high in the immediate vicinity of the parent tree, creating ideal conditions for specialist pathogens. These pathogens, the source of 'damping off' diseases, can wipe out all seedlings except those that have been dispersed far enough so as not to be at risk of infection. Such a process selects for seed dispersal. It also increases species diversity as the most successful seedlings are those that avoid being infected by being far from another tree of the same species. This process serves to prevent local dominance by any one species, and hence promotes species diversity.

This theory, first proposed independently by Daniel Janzen and Joseph Connell in the early 1970s to explain the immense diversity of tropical rainforests, has accumulated much support. Hence the effects of pathogens and other host-specific pests in tropical rainforests unfold on much smaller spatial scales than in temperate and boreal forests, and yet these small-scale neighbourhood effects play an important role in maintaining the great richness of tree species in many tropical forests.

Dynamics and succession

It is difficult for us to appreciate how dynamic forests really are. Forest disturbances, be they fire, windthrow, or pests and diseases, are often viewed as aberrations that belie the stability and permanence that is imbued in our concepts of 'old growth' forest. Indeed, the very stability and permanence of old growth forest underlies justification for their conservation in the face of disturbance by human artifice. Forests are not, however, stable and probably have never been so.

Even within human timeframes of years and decades forests undergo considerable, and often unpredictable, change. Disturbances also interact. A comparatively minor windthrow event, for example, creates a substantial fuel load of dead wood that favours a bark beetle outbreak or a devastating fire in following years. Pests, pathogens, or droughts also create dead wood and increase the flammability of forests, while surface fires injure trees and increase their susceptibility to pathogen or pest attack.

Disturbance need not beget more disturbance, and in some cases one disturbance agent can reduce the likelihood of others. For example, herbivores such as deer and moose create a 'fuel gap' between the understorey and canopy by clearing out vegetation in a two to three metre vertical space above the forest floor, and this prevents surface fires from spreading higher up into the canopy. The complexity of disturbance regimes might seem to make the task of understanding forest dynamics hopelessly complex. Long-term studies of forest ecosystems have, however, begun to reveal patterns in forest dynamics.

In contrast to many temperate forests, tropical rainforests straddling the equator are rarely, if ever, affected by natural fires, pest outbreaks, diseases, or stand-levelling windstorms. Rainforest dynamics are instead dominated by single tree fall events that create relatively small canopy gaps that saplings race to fill. In species-rich rainforests the successful individual filling the gap as a mature tree can belong to any one of many species, and so defining patterns of vegetation change in tropical rainforests is all but impossible in anything but a very general sense. Suites of 'pioneer' species—typically fast-growing, shade-intolerant, short-lived trees—that are the first colonizers of extensive open areas will be gradually replaced by slower-growing, longer-lived shade-tolerant species in a sequence that resembles the unfolding successional process in cold temperate regions, but it is hardly possible to predict which species will ultimately occupy the canopy in any one area.

In natural forests undisturbed by humans, single tree fall events account for the large majority of disturbances, and these are not extensive enough to allow pioneer species to become established. Yet catastrophic disturbances that substantially shape the structure and composition of forests do occur in seasonal tropical zones where wind and fire can be important, if infrequent, agents of change. The unexpected uniformity of ages, at around 150 years, of most large trees in Huai Kha Khaeng Wildlife Sanctuary, a seasonal evergreen forest in western Thailand, implies one such catastrophic disturbance dating back to the mid-1800s.

The variety of forest disturbances gives us an inkling of the complexity of change, but it is plainly challenging to make sense of all interactions among these processes to fully understand forest dynamics. Early theories of vegetational change are encapsulated within the concept of *succession*: the sequential development and replacement of plant species that gradually shifts a plant community to its final stable state, the 'climax community'. The many changes in Lady Park Wood over a relatively brief forty-year time span shows us that it is no longer tenable to think in terms of predictable processes driving vegetation towards stable forest states. Nonetheless, this concept of succession has long been a dominant model of forest development, and in a modified form it remains useful.

The successional sequence starts with the colonization of open ground, created by some major disturbance event, by individuals that arrive as seeds, or by sprouts from stumps or root stock. These young trees grow rapidly in the high-light environment until they begin to crowd each other and compete for light and space. Such 'pioneer' trees include aspen and jack pine in North America, birch in Europe, and *Macaranga* and *Cecropia* trees in the tropics.

As the canopy thickens younger saplings are shaded out, trees jostle for light and space, and there is a natural thinning of individuals. Surviving trees become bigger as they extend their branches into gaps created by dead or fallen neighbours. This stage might last several decades, but rarely more than a century. Eventually, trees become sufficiently large that when they die the gap created is too large to fill through horizontal extension. Light flooding into the understorey provides an opportunity for saplings and sub-canopy trees. Released from the shade of the canopy, they now grow quickly to fill the canopy gaps. These trees belong to a different suite of species that have been able to survive extended periods in the shade of the pioneer trees, growing very little but biding their time to the formation of a canopy break. They include sugar maple, hemlock, beech, and spruce in North American forests, or oak, beech, and chestnut in Europe.

These long-lived trees will eventually overtop and shade the pioneers. Mortality among them is no longer due to crowding but rather windthrow, with trees often succumbing after first being weakened by disease, a process that can take centuries to unfold. When a large tree does fall, dense clusters of shade-tolerant saplings that have been quiescent in the understorey respond quickly to the light streaming in and jostle for space and height. These youngsters are the progeny of the canopy trees, as pioneer species are long gone, having been completely excluded by the deep shade of the canopy.

The last stage of succession is the creation of a multi-aged canopy, resulting from repeated individual mortality events that are filled with younger trees growing into the canopy. If suitably ancient, this stage becomes synonymous with old growth forest.

This process of successional development has a feeling of inevitability to it. The early progenitors of successional theory, Frederic Clements and Arthur Tansley, accepted that major disturbance events could reset the process of succession, but disturbances were viewed as being exceptional to the normal state of events, that is the orderly and gradual transition to the stable climax community. In reality disturbances acting at several spatial scales play a more substantial role in forest dynamics than Tansley or Clements would allow. Taken together, these phenomena ensure that forest dynamics are usually neither directional nor predictable. Instead, a variety of pathways might be followed depending on the disturbance regime, local effects, and, more often than not, chance.

These pathways can be cyclical. Aspen is among the first to establish after a fire in cold temperate North American forests, but is gradually displaced by red maple and then shade-tolerant hemlock which persists until another fire clears the hemlock and aspen re-establishes. Successional pathways may be divergent: a post-fire aspen stand might succeed either to pine, oak, or maple on adjacent sites based on soil differences that favour different species. Pathways can also be idiosyncratic, whereby succession from one forest type to another is determined by chance events, such as the timing of major seed crops, or droughts or diseases that affect some species more than others. This model represents continuous non-directional change. Local processes, termed neighbourhood effects, such as seed rain, shading, nutrient inputs to the soil through litterfall, or exposure to pathogens from infected trees, all play a role in determining which saplings survive and which do not under the canopy of every tree. The sum of these neighbourhood outcomes contributes to the successional trends for entire forest stands. In the real world, predicting which of these models is most relevant, and projecting the composition of a forest into the future, is fraught with difficulty, as the recent history of Lady Park Wood reminds us.

Fire and the white pine enigma

This is not to say that we should give up on a more complete understanding of forest dynamics. Focusing on a particular forest type by way of example allows us to make the complex tractable. The cold temperate forests of the north-eastern United States serve this purpose well. White pine (*Pinus strobus*) cannot tolerate fire yet is, somewhat enigmatically, widespread in these forests where fires are prevalent. Unlike jack pine and black spruce (*Picea mariana*), white pine seeds are destroyed by fire. The tree also lacks the post-fire resprouting abilities of aspen and paper birch (*Betula papyrifera*). Mature white pine does, however, survive light surface fires, and tolerates some shading. Consequently, too much fire destroys white pine and favours resprouting birch; too little fire allows sugar maple (*Acer saccharum*) and eastern hemlock (*Tsuga canadensis*) to shade out the white pine. White pine persists in areas where the severe fire interval is between 150 to 300 years, sufficient to prevent the dominance of maple and hemlock, but not frequent enough to allow invasion by birch and jack pine. If the fire interval happens to exceed 300 years, the less flammable leaf litter of incoming maple and hemlock greatly reduces the likelihood of further fire. With fire largely excluded, windthrow becomes the dominant disturbance force. The recurrence of stand-levelling windthrow is on a cycle that exceeds 1,000 years, ensuring long-term maple and hemlock dominance. A repeating sequence of infrequent low intensity surface fires will, on the other hand, maintain white pine dominance for several centuries, until a severe crown fire provides the opportunity for birch to establish in the wake of the devastated white pine.

The white pine forest example illustrates that we can at least understand the processes at work even if forest dynamics are not obviously predictable or directional. There are exceptions though. The boreal forests of the far north do follow a reasonably predictable successional sequence, initiated by fire. In Alaskan boreal forests growing on peat soils, black spruce seedlings establish very quickly after a fire, and within thirty years a black spruce canopy begins to form. A hundred years after the fire a mature black spruce canopy is well established, but because fires recur at seventy-year intervals this stage is rarely reached. The recurrence of black spruce following frequent fires is a highly simplified form of succession where transition from one forest type to another is practically non-existent and a climax community is never reached as the fire interval is too short.

Deconstructing old growth

The complex and idiosyncratic nature of forest change, and the difficulty of attributing a 'stable climax' stage to any state of forest development, challenges us to question the meaning of 'old growth forest'. This term has been usually reserved for forests that are in the 'final' or 'late' stages of forest development. It should now be clear, however, that forests have no final stage except in the event of their complete clearance. Natural disturbances shape the course of forest development in an endless and indefinite cycle of change. Any forest stand will likely revert back to an earlier developmental state or shift to another state, subject to the disturbance regime it is exposed to. Old growth could instead refer to stages of forest development that are late in the successional development sequence following a major stand-levelling disturbance, but even this would need to encompass forest compositional change such as the shift from beech to ash at Lady Park Wood.

As succession proceeds, forests have a tendency to accumulate larger structures (both living trees and coarse woody debris), and increasing structural complexity (i.e. the three-dimensional variability in the distribution of biomass). The old growth forests of Boubínský prales in the Šumava Hills of the Czech Republic, the Białowieża Forest on the border of Belarus and Poland, or the temperate rainforests of the Olympic National Park in the north-western United States, are characterized by enormous fallen trees in various stages of decomposition, and several layers of regenerating seedlings, saplings, and young to maturing trees.

It is this structural complexity that ecologists often turn to as a defining feature of old growth. Minor and small-scale disturbances add complexity by creating a mosaic of patches that differ in successional development, and hence species composition. Old growth forests are therefore structurally complex, but also spatially heterogeneous at several scales. And yet a definition of old growth based on structural and spatial heterogeneity is not entirely satisfactory either, as some forests tend towards structurally simpler formations in the absence of major disturbances: without fire or windstorms, mixed hemlock/ maple forests of North America will, for example, gradually shift to either maple or hemlock dominated stands depending on soil type. From an ecological perspective it is therefore difficult to define 'old growth' in terms that can be applied meaningfully and unambiguously.

Ecologists, consequently, tend to use 'old growth' as shorthand for forest that is reasonably old and relatively undisturbed by humans, a concept that is more often intuitively understood than scientifically prescribed. In so doing, and whether they intend to or not, ecologists are adopting a value-laden social construct. This construct might not be universally held, and when agendas conflict, concepts of old growth forests can be at the heart of what becomes a polarizing political debate.

Old growth is thus viewed by some as being old, ancient, mature, original, primary, primeval, pristine, or virgin, terms that convey a sense of value worthy of preservation. This is challenged by others who might describe old growth in more negative terms, such as senescent, overmature, decayed, or wasted. This forms the basis of a discourse of conflict that takes us back to Julia Hill's two-year tree-sit: some view old growth forest as a suboptimal use of valuable tree growing land, while others see only a pure and natural habitat of great biotic and aesthetic richness. From a conservation perspective, old growth derives its value from its inherent complexity and rich biodiversity, which can be readily measured, as well as its visual and emotional appeal, which cannot. Disturbances of all kinds contribute to this complexity, and a healthy forest is also a dynamic one.

Chapter 5
Forest goods and services

A staple of Western mythology is first encounters of European explorers with previously uncontacted peoples. Such incidents are increasingly scarce, as few people remain untouched by the modern world. Yet Survival International estimates that over one hundred uncontacted tribes still live in tropical rainforests of remote regions of the Amazon and New Guinea, largely as hunter-gatherers and small-scale cultivators. Recognized examples include Bolivia's Yanaigua, Peru's Kirineri, Guyana's Wapishana (Arawak), Ecuador's Tagaeri, and Brazil's Karafawyana and Papavo. Other groups interact with communities outside forests, but continue to live as hunter-gatherers, including the Punan and Penan in Borneo, the Aka, Baka, and Batwa of the Congo Basin (Figure 23), and various groups of Amerindians in Amazonia.

We admire these people for their self-sufficiency and their sustainable use of natural resources, and contrast them with our own profligate exploitation of resources. Our fascination with remote forest tribes is, in part, a nostalgic romanticism for a simpler past grounded in self-reliance long since lost. Our increasingly urbanized modern society has distanced us, both geographically and culturally, from forest habitats. It is easy to forget that forests continue to provide many of the goods that we

23. Baka Pygmies in the forests of the Congo Basin.

take for granted, as well as environmental services on which our society depends.

Forest resources

Most obviously, timber is the main forest resource, and it is logging that sent Julia Hill to the top of that giant redwood tree in California. Her remarkable exploit was driven by the recognition that forests are far more valuable than their timber worth alone. Worldwide, some 1.5 billion people depend, in one way or another, on a great variety of forest resources for their livelihoods. Many millions more cultivate products such as coffee, rubber (Figure 24), and cocoa that are derived from or grown within forested habitats. Across the globe we all rely on many environmental services that forests provide, ranging from regulation of climate and the hydrological cycle to protection of soil resources, protection from hazards, as well as refuges for biodiversity and our own recreational, aesthetic, and spiritual needs.

24. Tapping a rubber tree in Sri Lanka around 1910.

Timber

Timber is, by far, the most valuable commercial forest commodity, with global trade values of wood products amounting to around US$150 billion. Timber has been the mainstay of economic development for much of civilization's history. It has been used for the construction of cities, ships, and railroads, and as such has generated the means to centralize economic and political power, through vessels for exploration, trade, and conquest, and networks for communication and control. Moreover, wood fuel (though not, strictly, timber) has powered human progress through most of our history. The expansion of Muslim powers into and across the Mediterranean in the 8th and 9th centuries was at least partially driven by the imperative of securing access to timber. The importance of timber as a resource is reflected in its use for political patronage in Europe through much of the Middle Ages. In Indonesia, Malaysia, and the Philippines rights over timber resources served to link heads of state, the military, and the private sector to create governing systems that shaped the economic and political development of these countries from colonial times to the present day.

Timber extraction, while often destructive of natural forests and their biodiversity, need not be so. Poor management practices and overexploitation continue to plague an industry that is, nevertheless, responding slowly to these challenges. Conservationists have long accused loggers of profligate unsustainable timber harvests that destroy natural habitat and biodiversity, displace indigenous and other local communities, and forever change traditional cultures. These arguments are now complemented by concerns over emissions of carbon dioxide from logged forests. Loggers counter by pointing out that logging provides an essential resource demanded by consumers globally, that the logging industry provides jobs and livelihoods to many thousands of people, and that logging does not destroy forests but instead imbues forests with economic values that justify their management and preservation. There is truth in all these arguments, and as usual the reality is more complex and nuanced than polarized ideological debate might suggest.

Logging alone does not cause deforestation. In the tropics it is a selective process in that only a few trees in every hectare have commercial value and are harvested. A logged forest is still a forest. In temperate and boreal regions it is more common to harvest all trees within a fairly extensive patch, a practice referred to as clearcutting (Figure 25). This is generally tolerable (depending on scale) as it reflects patterns of tree loss resulting from natural disturbance regimes driven by fire, windthrow, or pest outbreaks to which the forests are already well adapted and from which they can recover. The trouble arises when logging facilitates encroachment and conversion of forest to other land uses, something that might be actively or inadvertently promoted by government policies. The road networks that loggers leave behind are readily used by landless farmers or land speculators to access

25. Small-scale clearcutting operations in Ben More forest in Sutherland, Scotland.

logged land which is cleared for agriculture or ranching. In the Amazon, for example, logged forest is four times more likely to be cleared for agriculture than unlogged forest. Logged forests are also more vulnerable to fires which, in the tropics especially, can cause a gradual deterioration in forest structure and composition.

In Brazil, by far the largest producer of timber in South America, large-scale exploitation of timber was initially concentrated along rivers. As lowland forests became depleted of commercial stocks a large and growing network of roads penetrated into upland forest areas and opened up vast areas of hinterland to loggers. The pace of logging in upland areas is also likely to be unsustainable, but of greater concern is the penetration of the interior forests by roads that afford access to farmers and miners. A similar process has taken place in South East Asia where lowland forests of Malaysia and Indonesia have been logged and subsequently converted to agriculture or plantations. Calls for sustainable harvesting practices are loud and clear, but in practice they are rarely heeded on any significant scale. Most countries have well-developed forest policies and regulations, yet illegal logging accounts for much, perhaps most, of marketed tropical timber. High market demand, corruption at many levels, and difficulties in enforcing regulations allow the proliferation of illegal logging activities.

Can logging and conservation coexist? Can logging be made truly sustainable? Concepts of sustainable forest management differ, but they generally emphasize the continued existence of the forest and the viability of multiple forest products and services, including biodiversity, over the long term. The International Timber Trade Organization estimated, in 2005, that as little as 5 per cent of the world's tropical forests were being managed in a sustainable manner.

The irony is that methods and procedures for sustainable forest management are well developed and known. What are lacking are the incentives for implementation. The detrimental effects of logging on stand structure, biodiversity, and forest soils and services can be greatly mitigated by adopting reduced impact logging (RIL) guidelines. These guidelines comprise a series of management interventions that cover, among other things, careful harvest planning, refined workforce skills, site preparation, and improved technologies to minimize damage to soils and watercourses. Yet RIL is rarely adopted due to lack of interest stemming from poor enforcement of forest regulations, a lucrative illegal timber market, and the absence of long-term tenure necessary to encourage investment. The main barrier to adoption of RIL is, however, likely to be its high cost, which increases total costs of tropical forest operations by around 40 per cent.

These barriers are beginning to be overcome as environmentally discerning consumers are increasingly discriminating among wood products on the basis of sustainability. This growing market for sustainable wood products is reflected by the proliferation of labels certifying wood products from sustainable sources. Certification standards are set by certification agencies which might or might not be independent of the logging industry. Management practices of logging companies are evaluated against these standards by accreditation agencies. Certified logging companies can potentially secure a price premium for their products, thereby offsetting some of the costs of compliance. Probably more important to these companies is that certification helps them to maintain market share. Certification has grown rapidly in the past two decades, as reflected by a bewildering array of labels purportedly representing some minimal sustainability standards. Most certified wood is, however, derived from temperate forests and plantations. The Forest Stewardship Council (FSC), the largest international certification agency has, as of May 2014, certified 182 million hectares of forest worldwide, of which 52 per cent is boreal forest, 38 per cent temperate forest, and only 10 per cent tropical forest. Indeed, uptake of certification by tropical logging companies, where improvements in management and operational standards are most needed, has been limited. As of 2008, less than 0.7 per cent of remaining tropical and subtropical forests have been certified by the FSC, and less than 1.5 per cent has been certified at all by any accreditation agency.

The success of certification in promoting sustainable harvesting and management practices ultimately rests on the demand for sustainable products by consumers. Demand for such products in Europe and North America is generally high, but this is not yet the case in emerging markets. A massive increase in resource consumption in China has shifted the flow of tropical logs away from European and American markets towards Chinese markets. Chinese demand for tropical timber now far outstrips that of Western markets. Quite apart from the massive increase in demand, buyers in China are less environmentally discriminatory than their Western counterparts, which could undermine efforts to make tropical timber extraction more sustainable.

Moreover, the organization of the tropical timber value chain has changed, as China tends to import timber rather than processed wood products, which means that less value is captured by exporting countries and opportunities for domestic value-adding industries are fewer. The emerging Chinese market is undoubtedly having a disruptive impact on the organization of global wood-product value chains, and on the promotion of sustainable practices. These global trends are recent, and as China's economy matures it too may become more discerning in exacting higher environmental standards. If it does, we should expect rapid improvements in tropical forest management practices.

Non-timber forest products

Trade in forest products extends back thousands of years to the harvest and sale of camphor (sap from the dipterocarp tree *Dryobalanops aromatica*) and dammar, gum from several other dipterocarp trees. Indeed, these may be the oldest traded products. People living in and around forests, particularly in the tropics, have long recognized that forests provide a great variety and abundance of non-timber resources that are, collectively, often far more valuable to these people than timber itself. Fruit trees and medicinal plants were often given higher status than timber in early description of the bounties offered by the New World. London's *Moderate Intelligencer* noted in 1649 that in America a settler could be 'plentifully fed and cloathed with the natural Commodities of the Country, which fall into your hands without labour or toyle, for in the obtaining of them you have delightful recreation'. These resources include, principally, foods such as fruits and nuts, honey, and hunted animals, but also encompass medicines, building materials, resins, and poisons. People living along the Amazonian floodplain forests have been reported to use more than seventy-five different plants for a variety of purposes. Even this pales by comparison to Punan hunter-gatherer communities and Merap shifting cultivators in East Kalimantan, Indonesia, who have one or more uses for 1,457 forest plants. Many of these species and products have since disappeared from use (or disappeared altogether) due to drastic habitat modification and their replacement with manufactured items. Despite this, many rural inhabitants in tropical forest regions continue to harvest and exploit many forest resources for a variety of ends. Their expert knowledge regarding the natural history and values of wild forest plants is itself a valuable resource that might foster more enlightened development of forested regions, though such expertise is, sadly, largely ignored.

Poor communities tend to be disproportionately dependent on forest resources. For example, as much as 60 per cent of the cash income of Soligas tribal communities living in the Western Ghats forests of southern India is derived from non-timber forest resources. Some forest foods are collected infrequently and have little cash value so might not even be recognized as being important, yet they prove to be essential in offsetting seasonal food or income shortages and thus provide emergency sustenance, a form of 'natural insurance', during times of hardship.

Deficiencies in micronutrients afflict two billion poor worldwide. Forest foods can mitigate such deficiencies by contributing to dietary diversity, as is the case in Africa, where children living in heavily forested areas generally eat more fruit and vegetables and thus have more balanced and nutritious diets.

Most collected forest products are for local and subsistence use, but some are traded on regional and global markets and provide incomes for many rural people in the tropics. The fruits and young stems of açaí palms (*Euterpe* spp.) that grow in large numbers in low-lying areas of the Amazon estuary are widely traded across Brazil, while the international Brazil nut trade supports the livelihoods of thousands of Amazonian residents. Brazil nuts are collected from Brazil nut trees (*Bertholletia excelsa*) in natural forests, and the value of the trade has ensured the legal protection of millions of hectares of forests in Brazil, Bolivia, and Peru. Brazil nuts and açaí fruits together account for annual revenue of over $50 million in the Brazilian Amazon, rising to around US$70 million when other commercialized non-timber forest products are included. The combined value of these products is, however, dwarfed by revenues from timber (US$2311 million), which itself is only the third most important economic activity in the Brazilian Amazon after industrial mining and cattle ranching. Arguing for the protection of tropical forests based on the value of non-timber forest products, as many organizations do, remains challenging in view of the disparities in short-term economic gains.

Medicinal plants

The astringent, toxic, and bitter traits of many tropical forest plants signify their potential use for medicinal purposes. Remote poor communities in the tropics can ill afford to travel to public health-care centres, and even if they do there are the added costs of prescription medicines and doctors' fees to consider. Many people therefore continue to rely on the therapeutic properties, real or imagined, of wild forest plants, knowledge of which has been accumulated and passed on through many generations. Many forest plants are used to treat a wide assortment of ailments ranging from diarrhoea and fever to intestinal worms, snakebites, and, rather more prosaically, dandruff.

The pharmaceutical value of forest plants might prove to be one of their major assets. Both small and large pharmaceutical companies are prospecting for pharmacologically active compounds from tropical forest plants. As yet though, only a tiny fraction of forest species have been screened for their therapeutic values. Companies can be more effective by partnering with people who hold local knowledge of medical plants. People of Amazonian floodplain forests have, for example, long used the oily nuts of andiroba trees (*Carapa guianensis*) as an anti-inflammatory agent and insect repellent, and these nuts are now additionally being tested by pharmaceutical companies for their pain-killing properties.

It is often argued that the conservation of tropical forests is critical for humanity's ability to combat disease by virtue of the large stock of plants with as yet untapped pharmacological potential. The road from plant screening to the delivery of a thoroughly tested and commercially viable product is, however, a long one. Consequently, few of these efforts have succeeded and many of the smaller start-up companies have folded.

Bushmeat

While plants provide the bulk of forest resources, wild forest animals constitute an important part of the diets of many people in the tropics. Hunted wild forest animals (bushmeat) provide the main source of protein for approximately sixty million people across the tropics. In the Congo Basin alone over two million tonnes of bushmeat is consumed annually, and in the Amazon its value exceeds $175 million annually. Bushmeat also provides a 'safety net' during periods of seasonal shortfalls, particularly for people in extreme poverty who depend on forest animal resources to meet their most basic needs.

As human populations have grown, and as global trade networks have expanded, bushmeat has become a widely, and often illegally, traded commodity that finds its way into regional cities and towns and, increasingly, further afield to London and other major international cities. This is leading to overhunting in many tropical forested areas, facilitated by the ease of access to new forest areas created by logging roads and agricultural expansion. As people move into new areas, often as employees of logging companies, respect for local taboos on the hunting of particular species and traditional hunting seasons are increasingly disregarded to meet market demand. In some cases, forest animals have declined so precipitously that the phenomenon has been termed the 'empty forest syndrome'.

Many hunted mammals have important roles in dispersing the fruits of tropical trees, and so their loss could have long-term implications for forest regeneration and composition. Of immediate concern is the plight of Africa's great apes: the gorillas, chimpanzees, and bonobos. These constitute only around 1 per cent of bushmeat, but as ape populations are small even this represents a critical threat to their survival. Moreover, apes have very low reproduction rates, and are consequently not able to recover readily even from limited hunting.

Ecosystem services

Forests are credited with providing a multitude of ecosystem services—the direct and indirect contributions of forest ecosystems to human well-being. These benefits include climate regulation, flood control, pollution abatement, fresh water supply, and soil protection. Forests have been celebrated as the 'lungs of the world', pumping life-giving oxygen into the atmosphere, and as immense sponges absorbing storm waters and releasing them during droughts. In truth, natural forests are in approximate balance with the atmosphere, and neither add nor remove oxygen. The 'sponge effect' that is commonly attributed to forests has also never been confirmed, and despite much criticism levelled at it since the early 1900s it continues to appeal to many people (forest scientists included) and in many countries it has become firmly embedded in national forest policies and programmes. These apparent ecosystem services have also been readily co-opted by proponents of forest conservation.

Water quality and quantity

A prominent and widely cited example is that of the Catskill-Delaware watershed—in 1997 New York City committed to preserving forests through land acquisitions for the purpose of securing a clean supply of water. This ecosystem service concept is not new, even though it is often taken to be so. Indeed, belief in the capacity of forests to secure reliable water for irrigation and domestic use was a primary reason for the creation in 1885 (over one hundred years ago!) of New York's Adirondack and Catskills preserves. Similarly, in mid-19th-century Burma periods of drought were attributed to the deforestation of water catchments and inspired the colonial government to improve forest management. The prolonged flooding of extensive areas of southern England in early 2014 has rekindled the debate, at least in the UK, of the importance of forests for flood protection.

Forests use more water than other vegetation types. Forest canopies also intercept rainwater, which can reduce the amount of rainfall reaching the ground and thereby contribute to flood control. Coniferous forests are particularly effective at this and can intercept as much as 45 per cent of rainfall. Broadleaved forests also intercept rainfall, but in deciduous forests this benefit is lost in winter months when flood risk is greatest. Rainfall interception capacity also declines with rainfall intensity such that the amount of rain intercepted by trees during a particularly heavy rainfall event can decline to less than 10 per cent.

Forest soils are rich in organic matter. This gives them a more open structure, which delays the flow of rain water to streams and rivers and so reduces flood risk. This too has its limitations, though, as major floods tend to follow periods of exceptionally heavy and prolonged rainfall during which time forest soils become fully saturated and lose their capacity to store storm water. Forests do mitigate the incidence and severity of downstream flooding, but their capacity to protect us from particularly heavy or prolonged rainfall events is likely to be more limited than is often credited. Forests tend to prevent floods but, as Gifford Pinchot recognized in his *A Primer for Forestry* (1905), 'this good influence is important only when the forest covers a large part of the drainage basin of the stream. Even then the forest may not prevent floods altogether.'

Tree roots and leaf litter promote rainwater infiltration into the soil and then into groundwater. This has been assumed to improve water flows in dry periods. While intuitively reasonable, the assumption has been difficult to prove. In drier climates tree cover might be detrimental to water supply as rainfall intercepted by trees is evaporated back to the atmosphere before it even reaches the ground. Trees are also profligate in their use of soil water and can actually reduce surface flows to the detriment of downstream communities.

The jury is still out on the role of forests for mitigating floods and regulating water flows. Support for the sponge effect has been found in Panama where storm-water runoff from pasturelands is much higher than from forested land, and forests release more water during the dry season. Yet historical patterns of catastrophic floods, as well as droughts, reveal that recent deforestation has had no effect on the frequency of these events. Large-scale floods in the Chiang Mai valley in northern Thailand occurred in

1918–20 and again in 1953 when thick forests were still abundant. These complexities have not prevented people from attempting to value the ecosystem service benefits that forests provide. One such attempt estimates that the water storage function of China's forests is worth US$1 trillion, around three times the forests' timber value.

Soil protection and hazard abatement

Clearance of Mediterranean forests more than 2,000 years ago is said to have caused extensive soil erosion and land degradation. Yet it is not trees that prevent soil erosion, but rather the undergrowth and forest litter. Land degradation and soil erosion following forest clearance are more often due to poor land use practices such as overgrazing or burning that reduce litter cover and destroy soil organic matter. Mediterranean forest clearance during the Classical period was accompanied by extensive stocking of sheep, goats, and pigs, and it is more likely that overgrazing following forest clearance was the main cause of soil erosion, as is still the case.

In mountain areas rockfalls and avalanches are an ever-present threat. One of the main functions of forests is to protect people and infrastructure from these natural hazards (Figure 26). In Switzerland, 43 per cent of forests have a protection function, without which many villages in mountain regions would be uninhabitable. The Swiss municipality of Andermatt banned the harvesting of any part of their protection forests as long ago as 1397—it was even forbidden to remove cones from the trees. Protection forests work by acting as obstacles to the movement of rocks, snow avalanches, and landslides. Even dead trees on the ground limit downslope movement and can act as dams that hold back snow and soil. Protection forests can be replaced by artificial avalanche barriers, terraces, or dams, and often are when the effectiveness of the forest has been temporarily or permanently impaired, but the long-term

26. **Many mountain areas would not be habitable without the protection that trees provide from avalanches and rockfalls. This falling boulder has been stopped by a forest tree in the Swiss Alps.**

costs of doing so are estimated to be about 1,000 times that of forest maintenance.

Mangrove forests along tropical coastlines have a similar protection function, although in this case the hazards are storm waves and tsunamis. The dense root systems of mangrove forests trap sediments and stabilize coastlines against the incessant battering of waves (Figure 27). Mangroves reduce the destructive energy of a tsunami by up to 90 per cent. The effects of this were dramatically demonstrated by the 2004 Indian Ocean tsunami, when villages protected by mangroves suffered far fewer casualties than those that were exposed to the full force of the tsunami. The effectiveness of such protection depends greatly on the quality of the mangrove habitats, and degraded mangroves, of which there are many, provide far less protection.

27. **Mangrove root systems, here along the coast of Kenya, stabilize sediments and protect coastlines from wave damage and storm surges.**

Carbon storage and emissions

Forests store around 45 per cent of terrestrial carbon (25 per cent in tropical forests, 12 per cent in boreal forests, and 8 per cent in temperate forests). This carbon is held in plant biomass and in the soil, though the ratio differs among forest types. Most carbon in boreal forests is locked up in the soil owing to slow decomposition rates. Short cold summers and high acidity of conifer forest soils inhibit decomposition, and organic matter accumulates such that boreal forests average around 450 tonnes of carbon per hectare. By contrast, the carbon of moist tropical forests is distributed roughly equally between plant biomass and soil carbon as plant matter decomposes rapidly in the warm and humid tropical conditions and carbon is lost through respiration. Nonetheless, the productivity of tropical forests is high, and carbon stocks amount to around 270 tonnes per hectare. Temperate forests generally contain the smallest quantities of carbon, averaging only 170 tonnes per hectare, of which nearly two-thirds is in the soil.

While we once believed that carbon flows in undisturbed natural forests were in equilibrium, with the amount sequestered balancing that released, new observations show that forests are absorbing more carbon than they release and account for roughly half the carbon sink attributed to forests. Higher atmospheric CO_2 concentrations, as well as nitrogen emitted by industry, agriculture, and fossil fuel use, are fertilizing and accelerating tree growth worldwide. Yet many forests are no longer undisturbed, and tropical deforestation is an important source of greenhouse gas emissions. Each year conversion of tropical forests to agricultural lands releases immense amounts of carbon into the atmosphere which, apart from directly contributing to greenhouse gas emissions, degrades the Earth's capacity to mitigate anthropogenic emissions through forest growth. On the other hand, in both temperate and tropical regions many former agricultural lands are now experiencing forest regrowth, and these areas act as important carbon sinks. Active forest restoration has become a popular means to mitigate greenhouse gas emissions.

Climate regulation

Forests cast shade, transpire, and sequester carbon, and in so doing they help to cool the environment on local, regional, and global scales. Anyone entering a forest on a hot day will appreciate the cool air of the understorey, where the shade of the forest canopy provides welcome relief from the sun.

The movement of water through a plant and its evaporation from leaves, a process called transpiration, consumes heat and has a substantial cooling effect. On a sunny day, a moderately large tree can transpire around 200 litres of water, converting approximately 140 kilowatt-hours of solar energy into latent heat held in water vapour. As this moist warm air rises it cools, and forms clouds which precipitate rain elsewhere. This process resonates with the popular belief that blames deforestation for regional rainfall decline and even desertification. Most climate scientists ascribe relatively little importance to forest cover in determining global rainfall regimes, but attach more credibility to the role of forests in regulating regional climates. Forest fires have also been blamed for regional rainfall decline. Smoke reduces cloud cover by saturating the atmosphere with aerosol particles that bind water molecules and prevent the formation of raindrops. Large fires can consequently create rain shadows extending hundreds of kilometres downwind. Reductions in rain and mist in Costa Rica's Monteverde Cloud Forest, for example, have been attributed to the clearing and burning of lowland forest on the Caribbean coast.

The cooling effect of forest transpiration is counteracted by forests' comparatively low surface albedo, the reflectance of incoming solar radiation. This contributes to regional and planetary warming through the increased solar heating of land. Boreal forests reduce surface albedo in winter when snow on a treeless landscape would otherwise reflect much of the incoming solar radiation. Boreal forests therefore have a substantial warming effect on climate. Deforestation in the boreal zone could, therefore, contribute to global cooling. This is despite the fact that boreal ecosystems store immense amounts of carbon, accumulated over millennia, in soil, permafrost, and wetlands, which is released into the atmosphere as greenhouse gases following forest clearance.

Regional and global effects of temperate forest albedo are less certain. In the eastern United States the low forest albedo maintains a warm summer climate. The masking of snow albedo by trees in cool temperate North America also has a warming effect. The conversion of temperate forests to croplands has probably had a cooling effect on regional and global climates throughout history. The effects of albedo are, however, complicated by high evapotranspiration from forests (relative to croplands) that decreases surface air temperatures. Low albedo during winter and high evapotranspiration in summer influences temperature in opposing ways, and so the net climatic effect of temperate forests remains very uncertain.

Determining the net effect of forests on climate at various scales is fraught with difficulty. Many uncertainties remain about the processes that shape climate, and how different forests affect them. In tropical forests albedo-associated warming is more than offset by strong evaporative cooling through transpiration. This seems to be borne out at regional scales in Amazonia, Africa, and tropical Asia, where large-scale forest loss has often been followed by warmer and drier regional climates. The low surface albedo of boreal forests likely outweighs its carbon sequestration benefits giving a net warming effect on global climate. Least clarity lies with the climate benefits of temperate forests. Many temperate forests are undergoing expansion, and carbon is thus being sequestered in forest biomass, but the albedo and evaporative effects are poorly resolved compared to other forest biomes.

Forests can amplify or dampen climate change by the combined effects of albedo, evapotranspiration, and the flux of carbon. High rates of carbon accumulation in tropical forests augment strong evaporative cooling, but the continued benefit this brings to humankind is contingent on tropical forests' resilience to drought and the extent of deforestation. Many unknowns remain, including their role as carbon sinks, and the contributing effects of forest fires and the aerosols and reactive gases they produce, as well as the effects of deforestation on cloud formation and precipitation.

As the climate benefits of forests become better understood, land use policies can be crafted to mitigate climate change. Policies seeking to mitigate climate change by reducing greenhouse gas emissions through avoided deforestation must recognize that this is only likely to work in the tropics. The balance of albedo,

Forest goods and services

evapotranspiration, and carbon effects indicate that temperate forests have little net climate benefit, while boreal forests have a net warming effect. The spatial scale of these processes varies: greenhouse gases are well mixed in the atmosphere and influence global climate over long timescales, whereas biogeophysical feedbacks have a regional and more immediate impact.

Attenuation or amplification of climate change by forests will vary with global warming. As the climate warms and snow cover diminishes, the masking of snow albedo by boreal forests becomes less important. On the other hand, evaporative cooling by forests will decline as drier conditions develop. Huge uncertainties remain. Climate change mitigation policy requires that interactions among climatic changes, ecosystem responses, and human land use be addressed together if we are to comprehensively respond to these current and future challenges.

Biodiversity

On 26 September 1991, eight people were sealed off for two years within a glass enclosure little more than one hectare in size in the Arizona desert. This Biosphere 2 mission sought to test whether a system completely independent of planet Earth could support a self-sustaining human colony. Despite considerable planning and investment, and over 3,000 plant and animal species distributed across desert, savannah, rainforest, ocean, and mangrove biomes, oxygen levels in Biosphere 2 began to decline precipitously, vines began to overrun food plants, cockroach and ant populations exploded, while pollinating insects and most birds and mammals died out. Although the first two-year mission was completed, it ultimately proved impossible to maintain ecosystem services to provide adequate food, water, and air. The salutary lesson we learn from this extravagant experiment is that a rich and functional biodiversity underpins our global life-support system, and a diminution of this biodiversity, even if carefully planned, is no substitute for the richness and complexity of natural biodiversity.

It is in forests that most of the world's terrestrial biodiversity resides, and it is therefore forests that have attracted the attention of conservation scientists keen to maintain the goods and services that functional ecosystems provide. In truth, however, we have documented only a small proportion of life in the world's forests. Great extents of forest, such as the rainforests of New Guinea, have yet to be thoroughly botanically studied, so much so that we can only very roughly estimate the total number of vascular plants on Earth at something between 300,000 to 500,000 species. We know even less about how much of this biological richness we can afford to lose before suffering serious degradation in the ecosystem services on which we depend.

Nonetheless, limited knowledge does not prevent us from appreciating the value of this diversity, or from celebrating biological richness for its own sake, and for the sense of wonder that it imparts. I suspect it is this wonder that primarily drives our efforts to conserve forests, rather than concern over lost ecosystem services. Yet in our increasingly urbanized societies opportunities for first-hand exposure to the great diversity of forest life is diminishing. It is important, therefore, to remind ourselves of our global forest biological heritage.

It is, of course, tropical forests that most instil our sensibilities with biological wonder. Gorgeously produced picture books convey this wonder beautifully, but the reality is a little more hidden. It is true that tropical rainforests are immensely rich in plants, animals, and fungi, but it requires a trained eye to resolve the diversity of life. Many of the trees at any one location look similar, but where forests have been carefully inventoried the number of tree species ranges from well over 200 in a single hectare of Ecuadorian or Malaysian rainforest, to around sixty to one hundred species per hectare in African and Central American moist forests, down to between ten and twenty species in northern temperate woodlands, and as low as two to five species in boreal forests (Figure 28).

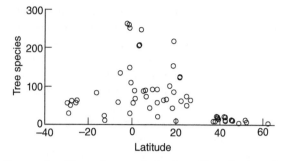

28. Tree species richness from tropical to boreal latitudes (negative numbers indicate southern hemisphere). Richness values are average number of tree species per hectare. Species diversity decreases at higher latitudes, but in the tropics there is considerable variation depending on forest type and locality.

This distribution of biodiversity from the tropics to temperate zones is similarly reflected by animal species diversity. In the western reaches of the Peruvian Amazon a dedicated bird watcher can, in time, record as many as 550 species within an area no larger than fifty square kilometres. By comparison, the entire 244,000 square kilometres of the United Kingdom can only offer the keen birder around 240 bird species. Tropical forests are also rich in mammals, where bats alone account for half of all mammal species. Second to bats are rodents. Bats and rodents together, although not the most charismatic of mammalian groups, are perhaps the most important functionally. Many tropical trees are pollinated by nectar-feeding bats, and many other trees have their seed dispersed by fruit-feeding bats. Other bats are superlative insectivores, catching as many as several thousand insects on the wing every night, which in the tropics helps to control malaria-carrying mosquitoes and agricultural pests.

Rodents consume vast quantities of seed, and by disproportionately predating the most abundant seed in any one place, they promote the persistence of rarer tree species and so contribute to the maintenance of high tree diversity in tropical forests. During times of plenty, squirrels in temperate forests, agoutis in the American tropics, and many other rodents worldwide, stash seeds in safe places for another day. Many of these seeds germinate before being recovered. Consequently, rodents are important if unwitting agents of plant dispersal, a process that is necessary for long-term plant persistence and which also maintains high tree diversity by removing seeds from areas of seed abundance where they are liable to be consumed.

Primates are what most people might hope to see in tropical forests. Almost all 270 primate species depend on forests across the tropics except for Australia and the Pacific. Year round fruit and leaf availability favours primates in evergreen tropical forests, and local fruit productivity appears to correlate well with local primate abundance and diversity. This preference for fruits makes primates good seed dispersers. Along with primates, the large cats such as tigers in Asia and jaguars in South and Central America are emblematic of tropical forests. Carnivores influence forest structure by keeping herbivore numbers low, which in turn allows tree regeneration. The loss of these large carnivores has already resulted in cascading changes that affect the structure and composition in both tropical and temperate forests. The extirpation of forest carnivores such as wolves, for example, has at least partly contributed to large deer populations in many European and American forests. The abundance of deer conflicts with human interests as deer kill young trees, injure mature trees, and, over a long period, change the flora and structure of woodlands markedly.

To a fairly good approximation, one in every two of the eight to nine million species on Earth is an insect in a tropical forest. Brightly coloured tropical butterflies spring to mind, and yet these are numerically and functionally inconsequential. It is the beetles that are particularly well represented in tropical and all other forests too, with over 350,000 documented species globally. While butterflies are pretty, beetles do things. They recycle dung and dead animal bodies, they disperse but also predate seeds, they pollinate many trees but also damage and even kill trees, they can be voracious predators of other invertebrates or more docile herbivores.

In terms of sheer numbers, ants dwarf all other forest insects. They alone account for around one-third of all insect biomass in the Amazonian rainforest. There are far fewer ant species than beetles—only around 11,000 globally—but again the very large majority of these occur in tropical forests. To place this in context, no more than fifty ant species are native to the entire British Isles, whereas sixty-one species of ant have been collected from a single tree in Sabah, Borneo, and ninety-five species from another tree in central Amazonia. It is, indeed, in forest canopies that ants are particularly abundant. This is surprising as ecological theory predicts that predators, which ants predominantly are, should only be able to sustain relatively small populations as they are limited by the abundance of their prey. Instead, it turns out that ants are able to support massive populations in forest canopies by protecting and tending sap-feeding insects from which the ants harvest exudates (honeydew). These insects therefore provide ants with their protein requirements (as prey) but also their carbohydrate needs, with ants acting as indirect herbivores.

Forest biodiversity is close to unfathomable to any great detail, and our knowledge remains highly patchy. We nevertheless know that forest productivity and the ecosystem benefits we derive from forests depend on well-functioning ecological systems. These are, in turn, a product of the diversity of forest species and the interactions among them. If this were not sufficient justification to warrant our careful management of forests, then the sheer wealth and beauty of forest diversity should provide sufficient inspiration to do so.

Chapter 6
Past, present, and future

The past: a history of European deforestation

Over forty years ago, Henry Darby, widely regarded as Britain's first and best-known historical geographer, suggested that 'the most important single factor that has changed the European landscape is the clearing of the woodland'. A human history of forests is largely one of deforestation, and is as old as human history itself. Hunter-gatherers leave fewer tangible marks on the environment compared to farmers, yet their effects on forests can still be substantial. Late Palaeolithic and Mesolithic people in Europe used stone axes to clear a little woodland around their homesteads. More importantly, they used fire to transform forest lands into heathland pastures to attract the wild animals they hunted. This practice was already long familiar to Australia's aboriginal people who have shaped landscapes using fire for over 50,000 years.

In Europe the destruction of wildwood continued through the Neolithic and Bronze Age (2400–750 BC), and intensified when iron axes and ploughs made forest clearance and soil cultivation easier. By 500 BC much of Europe had lost most of its original forest cover, and the Roman invaders of England (in AD 43) would have found a well-cultivated land. Roman industrial sophistication required specific types of wood supplies for a variety of purposes. Procurement of these supplies could not only have depended on remaining patches of wildwood which, apart from being greatly diminished in extent, could not provide consistently uniform products. Systems of forest management must therefore have been in place. This included coppicing, the periodic cutting of trees at ground level to stimulate regrowth of multiple shoots for poles, firewood or timber. Indeed, coppicing was first implemented by Neolithic people, since which time parts of the wildwood started to be transformed into managed woodland.

We know little of the people in the Dark Ages after the collapse of the Roman Empire, but the post-Roman population of Europe seems to have declined, perhaps due to plague, and forests might have recovered partially. The Doomsday Survey of 1086 reveals that England was not particularly wooded, with only half of surveyed settlements having access to woodland, and it is unlikely that any wildwood still remained.

The strong centralized states that became established in Europe from around 1100 expressed their power through the dedication of magnificent new cathedrals and castles, all of which required immense quantities of wood and timber for their construction. Moreover, wood was used for the construction of almost everything else, including houses and windmills, the latter even being blamed as early as 1322 for extensive deforestation in northern England. Growing populations also required more agricultural land. It seems that demand for timber soon outstripped local supply. In Lincoln Cathedral, England, built between 1190 and 1280, timbers used for the earliest completed roof sections were larger and from older trees than those used in later sections of roof, suggesting increasing scarcity of large trees.

Woodlands became a source of conflict between local populations, who sought woodland resources for their own needs, and sovereigns, bishops, and local landlords seeking to secure revenues from forest lands. Rivalries emerged between neighbouring towns and districts over access to wood. In pre-industrial Europe large-scale wood exploitation expanded rapidly from the 15th to 18th centuries to meet ever-increasing requirements including, notably, smelting iron to make axes and ploughs that, in turn, were used to clear more forest for agriculture. Multi-purpose woodlands were gradually replaced with more intensive single-purpose wood production to meet these needs, and short rotation coppice spread at the expense of high forest, first in Mediterranean regions and then elsewhere.

The first comprehensive description in the English language of the destructive impact of human expansion on the environment was George Perkins Marsh's book *Man and Nature; Or, Physical Geography as Modified by Human Action* (1864). Marsh did not challenge the right of humans to exploit nature, but he railed against 'profligate waste' and warned that 'we can never know how wide a circle of disturbance we produce in the harmony of nature when we throw the smallest pebble into the ocean of organic life'. 'Great political and moral revolutions' would be needed, he argued, to achieve the required 'geographical regeneration'.

Although Marsh's warnings were not well heeded at first, *Man and Nature* represents a turning point in European and North American attitudes to forests, particularly in recognizing the need for management to secure sustainable supply of wood products. In effect, this was the start of the now dominant environmental paradigm of sustainability.

The present: deforestation and reforestation

European deforestation presaged the recent deforestation of the tropics, which amounts to around twelve million hectares per year. The dramatic growth of global populations and economies, coupled with a massive expansion of global trading networks, has driven rapid and extensive tropical deforestation. More forests were cleared in the 1980s than at any other time in humankind's history, with the distinction that almost all this destruction was confined to the tropics. The decade of the 1990s was not far behind.

Tropical forest clearance is a familiar story that has been in the international media spotlight for many years, but deforestation is by no means a strictly tropical phenomenon. In 1998 catastrophic flooding along the middle reaches of the Yangtze River killed several thousand people and made millions more homeless. Deforestation was blamed, and soon after the Chinese government banned the logging of natural forests. China's wood merchants were forced to look elsewhere for their supplies. They turned to Russia. In ten years, from 1996 to 2006, declared exports of timber from Russia's boreal forest to China increased 38-fold (to over twenty million cubic metres). Chinese demand for timber is driving substantial deforestation in Siberia and Russia's far-eastern boreal forests, an estimated 50 per cent of which is illegal. No matter how far removed geographically, boreal and tropical deforestation still implicates European actors, as much of the wood that China imports is exported as cheap wood products to Europe and the United States, a process that contributes to the destruction of global forests, often to the detriment of some of the world's least privileged people.

Deforestation drivers

At its most basic, deforestation is all about opportunity costs: a forest will be cleared if the value gained by its conversion to other land uses exceeds the value of retaining forest as forest. A growing need for agricultural land is the primary driver of deforestation, as it has been throughout history. Essentially, agricultural land is more valuable than forest, and hence forest is cleared. This simple statement hides many ambiguities, not least how values are determined and which values are realized. Underlying social, economic, and political agendas influence land use values and the process of forest loss. Resource privatization, inflation-driven land speculation, and government agendas prioritizing rapid economic growth create opportunities and conditions that favour forest clearance.

Since the mid-16th century deforestation in the Brazilian Atlantic Forest was a direct result of settlement and investment in sugar, cotton, and coffee plantations and cattle ranching, promoted first by colonial administrations and continued by the Brazilian government. The assault on the Amazon began much later, and arose out of Brazilian economic development objectives, further driven by a political imperative to secure control over land, resources, and political boundaries.

Government-sponsored transmigration schemes to promote development of remote forested areas, also with an underlying agenda of security and control, have been prominent in South East Asia, particularly in Indonesia. Transmigration of people from densely populated inner islands such as Java, Bali, and Lombok to the outlying forested regions of Sumatra, Kalimantan, and Indonesian Papua became a pillar of government policy from the mid-1960s.

At supranational scales, globalized markets and fluctuations in regional and global economic health accelerate, and sometimes depress, deforestation activities. As prices of agricultural commodities increase, so does deforestation: the opportunity cost of retaining forest rises and therefore forest is cleared to plant more crops. A sharp rise in deforestation in the Brazilian Amazon followed the spike in global agricultural prices in 2008. Growing global demand for biofuels, including palm oil, soya, and sugarcane, has encouraged the exploitation of large blocks of forest for logging and subsequent conversion to agriculture (Figure 29). Economic recessions, conversely, lead to a slowdown

29. Forest clearance for oil palm development in Sumatra.

in deforestation rates as global demand for products wanes, and funds for agricultural investments dry up. Brazil's economic recession from 1987 to 1991 matched declining national deforestation rates over this period.

Despite the 2008 deforestation peak, by 2012 deforestation in the Brazilian Amazon had dropped by more than 80 per cent below the 2003–4 high. This has been attributed to macroeconomic trends, increased law enforcement, government policy, and private sector initiatives partly forced by pressure from environmental campaigners. This could signal the beginning of a transition to reforestation in the world's largest tropical forest. If so, the transition is unlikely to be smooth, with many episodes of deforestation and reforestation. Recent changes in Brazil's forest policy which governs how much forest a landowner must preserve, and an expanded push for new infrastructure projects could, for example, reverse some of the recent environmental gains, a possible indication of which is the sharp rise in forest clearing since July 2012.

Roads and rights

Government infrastructure and development policies hold central importance in influencing deforestation rates. Roads provide settlers and remote communities with access to resources, markets, schools, clinics, and other social benefits, but also accelerate forest exploitation and conversion. Who owns and controls forest lands is equally important in determining forest fates. Strong state control of forests in India has maintained forest cover in India's Western Ghats. Yet state ownership of forests in Mexico and Indonesia alienated people from their previously community-owned land and led to extensive timber smuggling and illegal land conversions.

Indonesia has awarded large forest concessions to logging and agriculture companies, resulting in the degradation of huge swathes of forest and conversion of forest to oil palm and low-grade wood plantations. Community-based management and secure land rights have been promoted as solutions to such ills. In Mexico the *ejido* system provides strong community ownership of land and resources, and usually leads to effective community-based management practices that preserve forests. Even the perception of tenure security, rather than the actual legal status of tenure, can be sufficient. In Indonesia, a decree issued in 1998 allowed Krui communities in Sumatra to register concession rights for their forests. The Krui communities never did formally apply for these rights, and yet knowing that they could provided the legal security for the continued preservation of their forests, while wide recognition of the decree has been instrumental in preventing outsiders from appropriating these lands. Of course, awarding land tenure to local communities might simply accelerate forest conversion which, for many people, offers a far more effective means to escape poverty.

Paying for forest services

Forests provide many ecosystem services, including carbon sequestration, climate mitigation, soil protection, hydrological services, and biodiversity. These values are not realized, or are at least they are not internalized in current accounting systems. It is not easy to quantify these values, owing to the complexity of demonstrating the real extent of these services and the manner in which they benefit society. Nor is it easy to attribute marginal values to the incremental loss of forest. Thus the value of some ecosystem services, such as carbon storage, decline linearly with forest loss, but others, such as biodiversity or water services, might show little response at first, but decline more rapidly, and sometimes suddenly and catastrophically, as forest clearance continues. Nonetheless, paying landowners for the services their forests provide has become a popular means to capture forest values. Payments for forest ecosystem services are designed to offset lost revenue from foregone land use activities.

One of the first such schemes, established by the government of Costa Rica in 1996, replaced an ineffective system of tax deductions for reforestation with a programme that provided payments to landowners for sustainable timber plantations and regeneration of natural forest on private land. The aim was to incentivize the provision of four ecosystem services: carbon sequestration, water quality, biodiversity protection, and landscape scenic beauty. By 2005 the scheme had supported the protection of almost half a million hectares of natural and regenerating forest.

In recent years similar schemes have spread to Africa and Asia. Most of these deal with hydrological services, but many carbon sequestration schemes have also been established through the Clean Development Mechanism of the Kyoto Protocol. The Madagascan 'Mantadia' scheme, for example, funds forest restoration for carbon sequestration and biodiversity conservation, and has soil protection as a secondary aim. The Chinese Grain to Green Program provides farmers with grain and cash subsidies in return for conversion of cropland on steep slopes to forest and grasslands to reduce water runoff, soil erosion, and river sediment loads.

International negotiations within the frame of climate change agreements have also promoted, though not yet finalized, a mechanism for reducing greenhouse gas emissions through avoided deforestation and forest degradation (REDD+), whereby payments are transferred from developed countries to developing countries that demonstrably reduce their deforestation rates. REDD+ adds value to forests based on their carbon storage service, but one of the biggest stumbling blocks is that market values for carbon remain too low to offset alternative land uses. This brings us back to opportunity costs. So long as forests are more valuable cleared than tree'd, local agents will continue to deforest.

Return of the forest

In 1955 Simon Kuznets postulated that as nations modernize income inequalities initially rise as labourers secure higher incomes from industrial and service jobs. After a time, inequality declines as the benefits of industrialization and the growing service sector diffuses out of urban centres to rural regions. Paralleling this process, an environmental Kuznets curve proposes that pollution and environmental degradation initially rise with industrialization, but later decline as technological and production efficiencies improve.

Forest transition theory draws on similar notions to argue that population growth and economic development initially drive deforestation, but forest loss is increasingly mitigated by urbanization and economic development through industrialization and agricultural mechanization. A transition point is eventually reached when forest regeneration begins to exceed clearance and forests recover, at least to some extent. The mechanism by which forest transition occurs is often conjectured to be rural to urban migration resulting in the abandonment of agricultural land.

This optimistic scenario is appealing in that it offers some hope for the recovery of forests, but how realistic is it? Alexander

Mather, a Scottish geographer, first formulated and championed the idea of the forest transition curve by drawing on the history of land use change in Scotland and later in other European and Asian countries. Forest depletion in Scotland has a long history, but by around 1500 forests covered little more than 5 per cent of land area, causing the Scottish Parliament of 1503 to declare the 'wod of Scotland is ... distroyit'. Laws were enacted to protect and rehabilitate forest, but to little effect. The transition came with extensive tree planting following the timber shortages of World War I. Lately, biodiversity, rural development, recreation, and carbon sequestration justify continued reforestation. Forest cover now stands at 18 per cent, which the Scottish Government aims to raise to 25 per cent by 2050.

Attributing forest recovery in Scotland to national economic growth, industrialization, and rural depopulation, as conjectured by forest transition theory, is not straightforward, as the proximate cause of the transition was government policy responding to a crisis of timber shortage. Yet land was available for reforestation partly because of depopulation of the Scottish Highlands over the preceding 200 years. Furthermore, competing land uses are limited, as agriculture accounts for less than 1 per cent of the economy.

The causal link between rural exodus and reforestation, as often described by forest transition theories, is more apparent elsewhere. In France forest area doubled from a low of 14 per cent in 1830 to the current 28 per cent, largely due to industrial development and urban labour shortages that drew people away from the land. This pattern was replicated in New England in the US, where almost complete forest conversion to agriculture since the early 1600s has been extensively reversed over the past 150 years following rural depopulation and industrial development. For similar reasons, South Korean forests have been extensively replenished in the past fifty years.

In the tropics deforestation remains the predominant trend, but even here there are indications that a transition to reforestation has begun. Since the 1990s forests have expanded in Bhutan, China, Cuba, El Salvador, Gambia, India, Puerto Rico, and Vietnam. Government policy appears to be an important factor driving forest transition. In China, India, and Vietnam forest policy and land use reforms provide incentives to landowners to restore degraded forests and invest in ambitious tree planting programmes. These policies grew out of an increasing scarcity of forest resources and, in some cases, disastrous flooding. This reflects reforestation policies of late 19th-century Switzerland and France, triggered by devastating Alpine floods. In both Puerto Rico and El Salvador, migration to the US in pursuit of better economic opportunities has facilitated reforestation in the wake of land abandonment either through depopulation or because many households have opted to cease farming and instead buy food using remittances from family members working in the US. Reforestation is a prevalent trend across the world, even as deforestation continues. Shifts to net reforestation are predicated on changes in the economic and policy environment, but each case is different, and attempts to understand forest cover trends through a single unifying theoretical framework have proved challenging.

The future: new forests

Forests are recovering in many regions of the world, but what kind of forests? The forests of New England are quite dissimilar in composition, structure, and variety from those of the pre-settlement era. The previously strong relationship between forest composition and regional climatic gradients is no longer reflected in the modern vegetation, which is more homogenous across its range. Secondary growth forest is, usually, less species rich and supports lower biomass than the original primary forest. Thus reforestation can support biodiversity and sequester atmospheric carbon, but is unlikely to fully replace that lost through deforestation. Many forest-dependent species become extinct in the course of deforestation, and invasive species that establish themselves in the interim can prevent re-colonization by native species.

Generally, the longer the period of forest loss, the more difficult it becomes to re-establish forest resembling that which is lost. Past land use history strongly affects the rate of recovery. It is more difficult to restore areas that have long been used for pasture or intensive agriculture than those used for short-term shifting cultivation, as soils, microclimate, and available vegetation can be very different from that which once sustained native forest.

Increasing forest scarcity drives up the price of forest products which stimulates planting. Forest expansion has therefore also been achieved by the establishment of plantations—artificial forests usually planted for commercial wood production (Figure 30). One-quarter of all industrial wood is currently sourced from plantations, which now constitute 4 per cent of global forest area. China alone claims to have established twenty-eight million hectares of plantations from 2001 to 2007, though this is contested. Plantations are not, however, substitutes for natural forests. They consist of one or a few tree species selected primarily for growth performance. These species are frequently not native to the areas where they are planted. Consequently, plantations are little more than tree crops providing few benefits for biodiversity or ecosystem services. Plantations do, nonetheless, produce much-needed timber efficiently and cheaply, and this could reduce pressures to log natural forests elsewhere.

Forest restoration, in contrast to plantation establishment, seeks to rehabilitate many of the original forest functions, as well as its biodiversity. Such projects in developed and developing countries are often supported by payments for expected environmental services. They often have the added benefit of facilitating community collaboration. In Tanzania for example, 350,000

30. A plantation of non-native silver oak (*Grevillea robusta*) established over a coffee estate in Karnataka, India.

hectares of acacia and miombo woodland have been restored by people from over 800 villages. In north-western Vietnam a group of villages have successfully restored natural forests by planting native trees, the consequence of which has been the recovery of water flow to rice fields and the return of over thirty rare mammals to the area. While such examples give cause for future hope, in most cases the resulting secondary forests remain deficient in species richness and ecosystem services compared to the original intact forest.

Future climates

Degraded secondary and heavily logged forests constitute around 60 per cent of global forest area. Given sufficient time, and if left alone, these degraded forests should recover naturally. Yet humans have changed the global environment such that the future of forests, and forest recovery, is less certain than it might have been. Plant growth is fertilized by higher atmospheric carbon dioxide concentrations and nitrogen deposition from industrial activities. On the other hand, higher temperatures and more frequent and severe droughts limit growth and increase mortality. The regions most vulnerable to a rise in global temperature of 4 degrees Celsius (a not inconceivable scenario) include the boreal forests of northern Canada and Russia, the savannah forests in the Horn of Africa, and the Amazon rainforest. Even wholesale dieback of the Amazonian forest is envisaged. Climate also influences disturbance regimes, often to the detriment of forests. Forest futures are further complicated by continued land use change, and are obscured by our inadequate understanding of vegetation, climate, and land use feedbacks.

Rising atmospheric CO_2 drives global warming. It also enhances photosynthesis and, therefore, tree growth, which sequesters carbon in plant biomass and helps mitigate greenhouse gas emissions. This effect can be substantial. Experiments have shown that a roughly 50 per cent increase in atmospheric CO_2

concentration enhances biomass accumulation by 23 per cent. While high atmospheric CO_2 concentration is good for tree growth, warmer temperature is not. Photosynthesis is first inhibited and eventually irreversibly damaged by increasing leaf temperatures. So long as water is available, evaporative cooling can keep leaf temperatures low. The problem arises when climate change limits water availability. Indeed, it is the increasing incidence of severe drought and chronic drying that is perhaps the most pervasive threat to future forests.

Severe droughts, such as the Amazon mega-droughts of 2005 and 2010, as well as chronic long-term changes in water availability in the Congo Basin, suggest that tropical forest climates might be shifting to new drier states. Remote sensing data indicate that forest productivity declined during the recent Amazon droughts, as it has more gradually in the Congo Basin forests. Some scenarios project that the combined effects of land use change, global warming, and increasingly severe droughts may shift the Amazonian region to a permanently drier climate, leading to wholesale Amazonian forest dieback and replacement with savannah vegetation by the end of the century. A warmer and drier climate can be exacerbated by deforestation and forest fragmentation which, at local and regional scales, further reduce moisture and increase temperature. As trees die the gaps formed in the canopy allow radiant energy to warm and dry the forest interior, while the dead trees fuel more severe fires. It is these interactions among ecological and climatic systems that might provoke Amazonian forest dieback.

Yet major uncertainties remain. The deep roots of many Amazonian trees draw water up to surface soils, maintaining high transpiration and photosynthesis rates for the whole forest ecosystem, but it is not clear how resilient this system would be to continued drying. Projections of drying of the Amazonian climate remain poorly resolved. Plants might adapt to warmer and drier climates, or at least forest composition might change to favour species best adapted to changing climatic conditions. Rising CO_2 might improve the efficiency of water use as leaf pores, through which CO_2 passes into leaves and water passes out, need not remain open as long. Alarming scenarios of Amazonian dieback remain credible, albeit unlikely.

While headlines proclaiming Amazonian forest dieback might be overstated, extensive forest diebacks due to heat and drought are elsewhere already well documented. Tree mortality has increased in tropical moist forests in Uganda and in mountain acacia woodlands in Zimbabwe. The El Niño droughts of 1982/3 and 1997/8 triggered widespread tree death in Bornean tropical rainforests. Recent droughts have killed pine trees across half a million hectares in east-central China. In Australia extended droughts have triggered widespread mortality of eucalypt trees. Europe has not escaped either. The hot dry summer of 2003 killed many oak, fir, spruce, beech, and pine in Spain and France. Scots pine is slowly dying back from drier Alpine valleys in Switzerland. Even the Aleppo pine, the most drought tolerant of all Mediterranean pines, was killed in large numbers during the severe drought of 2000 that afflicted Greece.

In northern temperate and boreal forests global warming is implicated in the creation of new disturbance regimes. Mountain pine beetles, normally contained by cold winter weather, now reproduce through milder winters leading to massive and extended outbreaks. In British Columbia alone more than thirteen million hectares of trees have been destroyed since 1990 by mountain pine beetle, releasing 990 million tons of CO_2 into the atmosphere (equal to five times the annual emissions from all Canadian transportation). Today the beetle occurs well beyond its historic range, having extended northwards and eastward into the boreal forests of the Yukon and Alberta. Moreover, droughts have weakened trees and rendered them more vulnerable to attack by beetles.

Climate change is also implicated in the pronounced upward trend in the area of burned forest in Canada over the last three decades. This presages predictions that annually burned forest area will double by the end of the century. In the western United States the annual forest burn area is already more than six times larger than it was forty years ago. Forests, even tropical rainforests, readily recover from infrequent fires, but climate change coupled with human land use is creating novel fire regimes that include more frequent and repeated burning. This can disrupt regeneration processes and cause dramatic and permanent shifts in forest composition and structure, even to no forest at all. There are precedents: a hundred years ago fires burned through 80,000 hectares of rainforest where the Sook Plain grasslands of Sabah, Malaysia, stand today. Extensive formerly forested areas of Indonesia are now dominated by highly flammable alang-alang grass (*Imperata cylindrica*), from which forest recovery is very difficult. Australasia, South East Asia, and South America might be especially vulnerable to the combination of human land use and drought, particularly as some climate models suggest a future of more intensive periodic droughts (driven by the El Niño-Southern Oscillation) in these regions.

From dry savannah woodlands to cold boreal forests to hot tropical rainforests, all forests are afflicted by global warming and, particularly, global drying. Is this a new trend? Past die-offs have been documented. The worst drought in Australian recorded history in the early 1900s caused the widespread death of eucalyptus and acacia trees. In 1915 New Zealand southern beech forests died back extensively. The American Dust Bowl droughts of the 1920s to 1930s caused substantial tree mortality in the Appalachian Mountains. There have been repeated episodes of drought-caused mortality of oak and pine in many European countries through the 20th century. So should we worry?

A cautionary tale that should give us pause for thought is the much hyped claim in the 1980s of impending forest death by acid rain in Western Europe and North America which, ultimately, proved unfounded (Box 6). Future drought exacerbated by continuing landscape transformations is undoubtedly an issue of concern, but widespread mortality of tree species and even whole forest stands is not a modern phenomenon, and neither can it be attributed to a single cause. Forest and tree decline, and their resilience and recovery, are complex processes. History shows that forests have weathered many earlier crises. Nonetheless, it pays to consider what steps we can take to ensure that they do so again.

Box 6 Environmental hysteria

In the 1980s *Waldsterben* (forest dieback) gripped the German nation. *Der Spiegel* ran a front cover story headlined 'The Forests are Dying'. Acid rain from industrial emissions was threatening the very existence of European forests. Only five years left, claimed the article. *Waldsterben* captured the public imagination, became a major election issue, and helped launch Germany's Green Party. Forests did not die back though. German forests are, if anything, expanding. So why the hysteria?

Acid rain coincided with an explosion of public interest in the environment. The German population was sensitized to suggestions of the contamination of nature, and particularly of forests, which run deep in German cultural lore. The impression of an emerging scientific consensus lent credibility to the phenomenon. In hindsight, there was no real consensus. The scientific literature was already replete with examples of species dieback in different places, at different times, and by many causes. And yet the intersection of an apparent scientific consensus, a media keen to capitalize on a dramatic story, and a politicized public convinced of the evils of pollution, all conspired to create a compelling but imagined environmental crisis. This is not to say that air pollution does not impair tree health—it can and does—but attributing large-scale forest dieback to air pollution alone is not, as yet, warranted.

Future management: resistance is futile

In managing forests we have a conception of forest ecological interactions and dynamics. These concepts are derived from historical, and often relatively undisturbed forest. Forest managers use this knowledge to set goals and inform actions. Yet we have now entered an era of rapid environmental change that has created conditions that have no precedent. We might have to manage forests in new ways, and the body of knowledge we currently possess might not be best suited for the purpose. Faced with an uncertain but certainly different future, we can either resist or accommodate change in our forests.

In the course of coming to terms with environmental change, forest management strategies have sought to forestall the undesired effects of change by improving forest defences. Interventions to protect against fire include raising awareness of fire risk, managing fuel loads, and creating fire breaks. Where invasive species become problematic they are removed. Pest populations can be controlled by herbicides. Biosecurity regulations can be developed and monitoring systems improved. Ultimately, however, resisting chronic environmental changes has been likened to paddling upstream: continued resistance to ever-changing conditions buys time, but is not realistic in the long term.

A willingness to accept change allows forest management to accommodate and adapt to new environmental conditions. Management and restoration goals could be rethought to allow gradual transitions to forest configurations better adapted to the new conditions. Success is not guaranteed and outcomes are uncertain. Among the practices being contemplated is assisted migration of trees along climatic gradients. Drought-tolerant provenances of pine from the Mediterranean are being introduced into Alpine valleys in anticipation of future drier conditions. Attention to, and conservation of, genetic diversity is a key component of this strategy. Increasing the diversity of forests in terms of both species and structural variety serves to spread risk and limit the extent of future disturbances.

We might also have to accept exotic species within otherwise native forest stands. This could require us to set aside the appeal of native species in favour of new forest communities in which exotic species are an integral component. Alien (non-native) trees can even create conditions that allow native trees to return. In Puerto Rico, for example, alien trees readily colonize deforested lands previously used for agriculture on which native trees cannot establish. A few decades later native species begin to appear in the understory, and a unique and rich community comprising both alien and native species slowly develops on these sites.

There are important lessons to learn from past forest dynamics. Nonetheless, we can no longer rely entirely on past behaviour to inform future forest management. Climatic changes, together with modern land use practices, are creating novel environmental conditions and disturbance regimes of which neither forests nor managers have much experience. We will need to learn as we go along.

Forests have weathered the depredations of human societies for millennia, and yet continue to provide many essential goods and services, and contribute less tangible but equally important recreational, cultural, and spiritual benefits to society. Far from being fragile and vulnerable, forests are highly resilient to disturbance and change, proving capable of regrowth, regeneration, and recovery even after complete clearance. Transitions from deforestation to reforestation have already taken place in many countries, and are underway in others (Figure 31). The future of forests is not in question.

What is in question is what kind of forests we will have. Conservative climate change scenarios project an increase in

31. Forests expanding once more over a landscape that had previously been transformed to cattle pasture in Guanacaste, Costa Rica.

global temperatures of 2–4 degrees Celsius, with significant drying in some regions, and increases in the frequency and severity of drought episodes. Such conditions are not unprecedented during the course of geological time, but the rapidity of change is. Moreover, humans continue to shape land use, creating novel habitat formations and landscape configurations. Interactions among climate change and landscape transformation are barely understood, but we know enough to realize that we should be concerned. We have created conditions in which novel disturbance regimes will proliferate. We have moved species across continents, inadvertently or otherwise, creating communities that are still sorting themselves out. Many tree species, and indeed many forest formations, will not respond sufficiently quickly to these new challenges. Extinctions will occur. Yet forests will persist. Only, they might not be the forests that we readily recognize today.

Further reading

Chapter 1: Forests in human culture

Cox, T.R., Maxwell, R.S., Thomas, P.D., and Malone, J.J. (1985) *This Well Wooded Land: Americans and Their Forests from Colonial Times to the Present*. University of Nebraska Press, Lincoln and London.

Frazer, J.G. (1894) *The Golden Bough: A Study in Comparative Religion*. MacMillan, London.

Harrison, R.P. (1992) *Forests: The Shadows of Civilization*. University of Chicago Press, Chicago and London.

Leigh, M. (2010) 'Lucan's Caesar and the Sacred Grove: Deforestation and Enlightenment in Antiquity'. In *Lucan: Oxford Readings in Classical Studies* (ed. Charles Tesoriero). Oxford University Press, Oxford, pp. 201–38.

Porteous, A. (1996) *The Lore of the Forest*. Senate (Random House), London.

Rackham, O. (1990) *Trees and Woodlands in the British Landscape*. Phoenix, London.

Williams, M. (1989) *Americans and Their Forests: A Historical Biogeography*. Oxford University Press, Oxford.

Chapter 2: Many forests

Ghazoul, J. and Sheil, D. (2010) *Tropical Rain Forest Ecology, Diversity and Conservation*. Oxford University Press, Oxford.

Henry, J.D. (2002) *Canada's Boreal Forest*. Smithsonian Institution Scholarly Press, Washington, DC.

Perry, D.A., Oren, R., and Hart, S.C. (2008) *Forest Ecosystems* (2nd edition). Johns Hopkins University Press, Baltimore.

Peterken, G.F. (1996) *Natural Woodland: Ecology and Conservation in Northern Temperate Regions*. Cambridge University Press, Cambridge.

Primack, R. and Corlett, R. (2005) *Tropical Rain Forests: An Ecological and Biogeographical Comparison*. Blackwell Publishing, Oxford.

Rackham, O. (2006) *Woodlands*. New Naturalist Library (100). Collins, London.

Turner, I.M. (2001) *The Ecology of Trees in the Tropical Rain Forest*. Cambridge University Press, Cambridge.

Chapter 3: Forest origins

Beerling, D. (2007) *The Emerald Planet*. Oxford University Press, Oxford.

Morely, R.J. (2000) *Origin and Evolution of Tropical Rain Forests*. John Wiley & Sons, Chichester.

Willis, K.J. and McElwain, J.C. (2002) *The Evolution of Plants*. Oxford University Press, Oxford.

Chapter 4: Disturbance and dynamics

Carson, W.P. and Schnitzer, S.A. (eds) (2008) *Tropical Forest Community Ecology*. John Wiley & Sons, Chichester.

Chapin III, F.S., Oswood, M.W., van Cleve, K., Viereck, L.A., and Verbyla, D.L. (eds) (2006) *Alaska's Changing Boreal Forest*. Oxford University Press, Oxford.

Frehlich, L.E. (2002) *Forest Dynamics and Disturbance Regimes: Studies from Temperate Evergreen-Deciduous Forests*. Cambridge University Press, Cambridge.

Whelan, R.J. (1995) *The Ecology of Fire*. Cambridge University Press, Cambridge.

Chapter 5: Forest goods and services

Bauhus, J., van der Meer, P., and Kanninen, M. (eds) (2010) *Ecosystem Goods and Services from Plantation Forests*. Earthscan, Abingdon.

Daily, G.C. (ed.) (1997) *Nature's Services: Societal Dependence on Natural Ecosystems*. Island Press, Washington, DC.

Pagiola, S., Bishop, J., and Landell-Mills, N. (2002) *Selling Forest Environmental Services: Market-Based Mechanisms for Conservation and Development*. Earthscan, London.

Chapter 6: Past, present, and future

Chazdon, R. (2014) *Second Growth: The Promise of Tropical Forest Regeneration in an Age of Deforestation*. University of Chicago Press, Chicago and London.

Dauvergne, P. (2001) *Loggers and Degradation in the Asia-Pacific: Corporations and Environmental Management*. Cambridge University Press, Cambridge.

Gawthorp, D. (2000) *Vanishing Halo: Saving the Boreal Forest*. Greystone Books, Vancouver.

Laurance, W.F. and Peres, C.A. (2006) *Emerging Threats to Tropical Forests*. University of Chicago Press, Chicago and London.

Malhi, Y. and Phillips, O. (2005) *Tropical Forests and Global Atmospheric Change*. Oxford University Press, Oxford.

Rudel, T.K. (2005) *Tropical Forests: Regional Paths of Destruction and Regeneration in the Late Twentieth Century*. Colombia University Press, New York.

Williams, M. (2003) *Deforesting the Earth: From Prehistory to Global Crisis*. University of Chicago Press, Chicago and London.

Index

Forests

Index

Forests